The High Stakes of Testing

Constructing Knowledge: Curriculum Studies in Action

Series Editors

Brad Porfilio (*Seattle University, USA*)
Julie Gorlewski (*Virginia Commonwealth University, USA*)
David Gorlewski (*Virginia Commonwealth University, USA*)

Editorial Board

Sue Books (*State University of New York at New Paltz, USA*)
Ken Lindblom (*Stony Brook University, New York, USA*)
Peter McLaren (*Chapman University, Orange, USA*)
Wayne Ross (*University of British Columbia, Canada*)
Christine Sleeter (*California State University, Monterey, USA*)
Eve Tuck (*Ontario Institute for Studies in Education,
University of Toronto, Canada*)

VOLUME 19

The titles published in this series are listed at *brill.com/ckcs*

The High Stakes of Testing

Exploring Student Experience with Standardized Assessment through Governmentality

By

Amy L. Kelly

BRILL
SENSE

LEIDEN | BOSTON

All chapters in this book have undergone peer review.

The Library of Congress Cataloging-in-Publication Data is available online at http://catalog.loc.gov

Typeface for the Latin, Greek, and Cyrillic scripts: "Brill". See and download: brill.com/brill-typeface.

ISSN 2213-722X
ISBN 978-90-04-40134-1 (paperback)
ISBN 978-90-04-38723-2 (hardback)
ISBN 978-90-04-40136-5 (e-book)

Copyright 2019 by Koninklijke Brill NV, Leiden, The Netherlands.
Koninklijke Brill NV incorporates the imprints Brill, Brill Hes & De Graaf, Brill Nijhoff, Brill Rodopi, Brill Sense, Hotei Publishing, mentis Verlag, Verlag Ferdinand Schöningh and Wilhelm Fink Verlag.
All rights reserved. No part of this publication may be reproduced, translated, stored in a retrieval system, or transmitted in any form or by any means, electronic, mechanical, photocopying, recording or otherwise, without prior written permission from the publisher.
Authorization to photocopy items for internal or personal use is granted by Koninklijke Brill NV provided that the appropriate fees are paid directly to The Copyright Clearance Center, 222 Rosewood Drive, Suite 910, Danvers, MA 01923, USA. Fees are subject to change.

This book is printed on acid-free paper and produced in a sustainable manner.

Contents

Acknowledgements VII

1 **Introduction: Who Cares What the Kids Think?** 1
   National Turn toward Testing 4
   Critical Pedagogy 6

2 **Understanding High-Stakes Standardized Exams in the US** 15
   The History 15
   Pearson 20
   Consequences 22

3 **What Is Student Voice?** 26
   Context 26
   In Research 27
   In Practice 29

4 **How Foucault's Governmentality Can Help** 33
   The Theory 33
   In Research 39
   For Student Voice and Testing 44

5 **The Study** 49
   Methods 49
   Means 53

6 **What the Kids Have to Say** 59
   By Grade Level 60
   Their Big Ideas 69

7 **Interpreting Student Voice: Themes** 76
   Adverse Attitudes, Feelings, and Experiences with Testing Practices 77
   Purposes and Consequences of Standardized Assessments 82
   Standardized Tests as a Means to Normalize Student Populations 86
   The Ways in Which Students Exhibit Obedience 90
   Student References to a Hierarchy of Power and Control in Schools 93
   Technologies of the Self 96

Grade Eight Theme: Resistance   98
   Change over Time   102
   Summary   105

8 **What Does All This Mean?**   106
   Recapitulation   106
   Conclusions   107
   Recommendations   116

9 **Possibilities: Where Do We Go from Here?**   118
   Opting-Out   119
   Alternatives   120
   Reflections   123

   References   125
   Index   133

Acknowledgements

This work is dedicated to *all* public school children, especially my past and future students; I believe in you, I trust you, and I am listening to you.

To my incredible husband, Brian, who believed in me even when I didn't believe in myself. Thank you for being my everything, I could not have done this without you. All my love.

To my beautiful daughters, Charlotte and Shea, and my adoring son, Jack; you are and always will be my inspiration. Mommy loves you more than you will ever know.

To my amazing Mom and Dad, thank you for instilling determination, perseverance, and optimism. Your unconditional love and support can get me through anything.

To the faculty at Lewis University's Doctor of Education Department and my dissertation committee, Dr. Lauren Hoffman, Dr. William Reynolds and Dr. Brad Porfilio, thank you for your committed support. I am truly appreciative of your guidance and insight.

To the Brill Sense *Constructing Knowledge: Curriculum Studies in Action* series editors Brad Porfilio, Julie Gorlewski, David Gorlewski, and the editorial board, Sue Books, Ken Lindblom, Peter McLaren, Wayne Ross, Christine Sleeter, and Eve Tuck, who have given me the opportunity to share this work in their series and broaden the conversation about the failure of standardized testing and the importance and urgency of student voice work in education.

To my family, friends, colleagues, and students, your help and encouragement has been invaluable as I have embarked on this labor of love. I am indebted to my school's administration who allowed me to conduct my research. And above all, I thank the seven students who participated in this study. I truly value your time, your thoughts, and your voices.

CHAPTER 1

Introduction: Who Cares What the Kids Think?

> *Dialogue is a way of knowing and should never be viewed as a mere tactic to involve students in a particular task...dialogue presents itself as an indispensable component of the process of both learning and knowing?*
> FREIRE (2010, p. 17)

∴

The first experience I can remember with high-stakes standardized testing was in the summer before third grade. It was a steamy July day as I headed to the intermediate building with my mom to participate in a one-on-one test, which would determine whether or not I was to be enrolled in the "gifted" third grade classroom the following fall. I recall an anxiety about the entire experience, partially about entering this intimidating building where the big kids went to school and the other part about...the test. This wasn't like a reading selection test or sight word test or weekly spelling test. This was different and it was *important*!

The apprehension of participation in an assessment of that nature is a significant part of the educative experience for public school children across the United States. The many symptoms of test stress among young children, include nausea, crying, panic attacks, tantrums, headaches, sleeplessness, depression, and refusal to go to school (Schaeffer, 2018). My first-hand experience as a test-taker and eventually test-administrator confirms these adverse effects. And while these negative consequences are well-documented, we continue to require students to participate in yearly exams. Their prevalence and pervasiveness leads students to view district tests, state tests, entrance, and exit exams as an organic part of public schooling in the United States.

In this book, I explore the ways that students experience standardized testing in public school through observations and interviews. Historically, students have been excluded from conversations about the very policies and practices that affect them. "By looking at students as subjects that lack agency and voice, we undermine their role as agents of change and as partners in shaping equity-based reform" (Diera, 2016, p. 232). It is my hope, that giving students a space to have their voices heard and sharing what they have to say, we will encourage positive social transformation.

I designed and executed a critical qualitative case study to consider the ways that students perceive standardized testing. Critical research investigates relationships of power and seeks to bring about change by challenging the social structures in place that marginalize certain populations. I view standardized testing practices through a critical lens. I believe, that these high-stakes assessments are bias and oppressive to culturally, linguistically, and academically diverse students as well as those from low-income families. My research grew from my personal experience with yearly state-wide exam administration as a public school teacher.

I began my teaching career right out of college in a low-income suburb of a Midwestern city as an intermediate self-contained cross-categorical special education teacher. Intermediate in our district refers to third, fourth, and fifth graders of which I had all three in my class of six students. This also meant that they would be required to take the state achievement test in March as all students beginning in grade three through grade eight must participate. The students I had in my class that first year were wonderful, they were kind and inquisitive, they were genuine and smart. They were also labeled with disabilities ranging from autism to learning disability to behavioral disorder and many, if not all were performing well below grade level in academic areas such as reading, writing, and mathematics. Regardless, they would endure grade-level standardized tests come Spring and there was nothing I could do about it. I would have to watch my students who perhaps read at a first grade level struggle with a test written for a fifth grade student. I was not able to help or assist them in any way. To me, this practice was unfair, illogical, and wasteful.

Assessment should guide instruction. As educators, we are constantly (informally) assessing our students. Asking questions, observing, exit slips, practice problems, and conversations are all forms of formative assessments. Arguably, data collected through those natural means influences our practice the most; helps us meet the needs of our students and make meaningful connections. To the contrary, statewide summative achievement exams cannot possibly assist teachers in planning instruction based on their students' achievement. To begin, this high-stakes summative grade level test is typically administered over two months prior to the end of the school year. Many educators, myself included, feel the pressure to rush through tested content in an effort to give their students a better advantage on the test. "The fundamental purpose of assessment is gathering information that leads to improvement in students' competencies in relevant domains of behavior and achievement. If assessment practices do not do so, *they do not matter*" (Salvia, Ysseldyke, & Witmer, 2017, p. 11).

The next eight years of my elementary teaching career were spent in a general education third grade classroom, where I learned the standards, the curriculum, the *assessments*, and what it meant to be a third grader and a third grade teacher in the state. I have always thought third graders are the perfect age to teach; they are smart, self-sufficient, and they love their teachers. Perhaps the only real problem I have with third grade is that it is the beginning of their standardized testing career for the state. I have actually had students come in on the first day of school nervous about "the test" coming at end of the year. My thoughts were always, "how could they know?" "Who or what is emphasizing the significance of the test?" And of course, "how can I, as their teacher, ease their anxiety?"

Following the state's adoption of Common Core State Standards the Partnership for Assessment of Readiness for College and Careers (PARCC) test was adopted. The previous statewide exam was always extremely difficult for most students; the difficulty of the format, the length etc. but it was accessible. The PARCC, on the other hand, was impervious; with seemingly never-ending reading passages only to be followed by a handful of questions, EBSR questions (Evidence-Based Selected-Response), extended response items, math questions that appeared to be assessing reading ability rather than an arithmetic concept, and this test was to be completed entirely on an electronic device. It was agonizing to watch my kids struggle with this test knowing there was nothing I could do to help. Around this time our district administration changed and so did the pressure to increase student performance on the PARCC as well as the other district-wide standardized assessments. My animosity and resistance to these oppressive testing practices inspired my research. I offer the preceding narrative to provide context and an understanding of the foundation upon which the rest of this book sets.

Through the next nine chapters, I will unpack standardized assessment as experienced by seven students in public education through a governmentality lens and draw upon tenets of critical pedagogy. For the remainder of this first chapter, I will briefly share the recent growth of testing in schools as well an in-depth discussion of critical pedagogy and how this theory informed the design of my research. Chapter 2 continues with a comprehensive exploration of high-stakes standardized exams in the US including the history and consequences for both students and teachers.

Chapter 3 considers student voice work as a fundamental component of this research. I begin by providing context for student voice work followed by an extensive review of student voice work in research and practice. Chapter 4 concerns Foucault's theory of governmentality and its influence and impact on student voice and testing. The methods and means of the study are reviewed in Chapter 5.

Chapters 6 and 7 consider what the kids have to say about their experiences with standardized testing. I present these ideas by student, by grade level, and by interpreting themes that emerged upon analysis. Six common themes of standardized assessment practice in public schools developed from this research: (1) adverse attitudes, feelings, and experiences with testing practices, (2) purposes and consequences of standardized assessments, (3) the ways that standardized tests are used to normalize through labeling and sorting student populations, (4) the ways in which students exhibit obedience, (5) student references to a hierarchy of power and control in schools, and (6) Technologies of the Self.

In Chapter 8, I examine the data to draw conclusions. The six themes are greatly informed by governmentality and suggest that students are manipulated, regulated, and disciplined to view standardized testing as a natural part of what it means to be a public school student. This is somewhat expected as "the average student in America's big-city public schools takes some 112 mandatory standardized tests between pre-kindergarten and the end of 12th grade—an average of about eight a year" (Strauss, 2015). Additionally, the data provides insight into the arbitrary nature of the preparation and practice students endure prior to taking these tests in school. Finally, this research shows that meaningful, deliberate, continued student voice work needs to be a part of the student experience in school. Finally, in Chapter 9, I propose future possibilities for the disciplines of student voice work and standardized assessment, which includes opting-out of statewide testing and alternative formats to these exams. As you will read, there are many negative aspects of high-stakes assessment but we can find hope by listening to our students' voices.

National Turn toward Testing

Education reforms generate an *"image of stability"* whereby there is an illusion of progress especially when these reforms are connected to "documentation of improvement, such as test scores" (Sonu, Gorlewski, & Vallée, 2016, p. 5). The turn toward testing for accountability in recent years is not strictly limited to the United States. There has been a global transformation, not only types of assessments but in quality and outcomes. Traditionally, the high-stakes attached to exams determined students' academic and career paths (Smith, 2014, p. 5). It could be argued that the outcomes remain quite similar today. With federal legislation that mandates standardized assessments and harsh consequences attached, the stakes are very high for children, teachers, administrators, and public education systems in the United States.

Accountability measures have a long history in the United States and continue to be perpetuated through legislative measures, most recently the reauthorization of the Elementary and Secondary Education Act (ESEA) under the name Every Student Succeeds Act (ESSA). Student voice remains in the periphery both in reference to education research and as practice within the classroom setting. Howard (2001) assents, "If the programs, practices, and policies rendered within the framework of the places called schools are delivered with students' best interest in mind, we must ask why their voices are so blatantly omitted" (p. 132). The ever-increasing standardized testing culture of schools and the lack of student input in educational decisions make this study both significant and necessary.

The primary purpose of this work is to raise awareness of student experiences and perspectives of standardized testing. Forty-two states and the District of Columbia have adopted the Common Core State Standards and the remaining states have established their own standards to comply with No Child Left Behind (NCLB). Because universal standards exist, accountability measures are in place to sort and rank America's youth. Standardized assessments serve such purposes and in my state students in grades three, four, five, six, seven, eight and once again in high school are required to participate in the Partnership for Assessment of Readiness for College and Careers (PARCC) test.

This work was designed to be significant for students, teachers, administrators, parents, teacher education candidates, and all those who have a stake in public education. In 2010 there were 22 states across the US aligned with PARCC, now remain only seven fully-participating states including this Midwestern state (parcconline.org, 2017). The significant decline in utilization and affiliation can be directly attributed to the widely publicized problems associated with the PARCC test across the country.

There are a wealth of studies and educational research that highlight the negative effects and consequences of standardized testing practices (Amrein & Berliner, 2002; Cormack & Comber, 2013; Hout, Elliott, & Frueh, 2012; Jolley, 2014; Jones & Egley, 2007; Leistyna, 2007; Minarechová, 2012). While the problems with such standardized assessment measures are widely researched and exposed, the tests remain in schools around the world. Dorn (2003) and Hillocks (2002) argue "that high stakes assessments serve to perpetuate current class structures by maintaining skill gaps and controlling ideology, particularly beliefs in individualism, meritocracy, and what counts as knowledge" (as cited in Gorlewski, 2012, p. 226). This study aims to give students the opportunity to have their voices heard regarding how they feel. These students are required to endure futile, standards-fueled public education *and* participate in the tests. I believe that allowing students to discuss these practices in a safe and honest environment is a way to promote justice and equality in schools. I hope that this work sheds light upon the ineffectuality of tests like the PARCC and advocates for the utility and benefit of student participation in educational research.

Finally, it is crucial to prepare students as future global citizens who will question, pushback and not become passive, docile individuals. Accepting the inevitably of phenomena such as standardized assessments without reflection is dangerous. I passionately believe that kids can and should have a more prominent role in education. It is my hope that by helping students reveal their voice through educational research, we will find better prepared, well-informed, critical adults in our society.

The 2010 emergence of the Common Core State Standards demanded that schools dictate unified content and measure understanding through aligned assessments. While the national turn toward testing and standardization is a modern topic of conversation, this educative process is nothing new in the US. In the 1890's a group known as the Committee of Ten claimed education was failing, similar to our governors today. Specifically, this group cited that students in college lacked skills and habits they should have acquired as children (Thomas, 2012, p. 56). To resolve this problem, the group suggested an eerily similar solution. When it is suggested by those with power that students are unsuccessful it projects the image that schools are failing. Consequently, outside entities (the Committee of Ten, US Governors, etc.) charge themselves with the task of remedying school failure through standards and related assessments. This cycle of prescriptive content and measurement of acquiring said content has been unsuccessful time and time again (Thomas, 2012, p. 56).

Critical Pedagogy

Freire's critical pedagogy has largely influenced the ways in which I have approached my work. Critical pedagogy is a complex notion and requires great effort and dedication from the educators who practice it. Kincheloe (2008) identifies a dozen central characteristics of critical pedagogy. In the following section, I will address these central characteristics. As my work primarily focuses upon public education, the coming discussion will be concentrated in this area, specifically addressing schools, teachers, and administrators. I explore this through the critical pedagogical aspects as described by Kincheloe (2008). I believe viewing critical pedagogy in this way provides a deeper understanding of how and why this theory could and should be used in schools as well as why it is influential to my work. The dominant discourses of student voice have been established within a democratic and participatory

INTRODUCTION 7

framework (Taylor & Robinson, 2009, p. 164). This type of framework is fundamentally critical, which is ideal for my purposes.

"Critical Pedagogy is grounded on a social and educational vision of justice and equality" (Kincheloe, 2008, p. 6). In this context, the critical educator views schooling as one aspect of a larger set of human services. This larger vision of schooling assists teachers in figuring out how they can empower students to be critical, global citizens (Kincheloe, 2008, pp. 7–8). Critical pedagogy means having a global conscious, being a citizen of the world, and loving and caring for the world and the fellow man. Global consciousness sprouts from understanding one's interconnectedness between the self and the world. Construction of a positive self-identity relies on relations between the self and others. Learning about the self as well as the vast diversity in the world allows one to contribute in a democratic society. "The ability to ally ourselves with others who may be very different in needs, perspectives, or background is fundamental to an ability to understand and to participate fully in the world around us" (Shields, 2013, p. 96). This global education needs to begin young; teachers should incorporate lessons about economic, ecologic, and social justice issues. Children are capable of comprehending the complex interconnectedness to the world. Globally conscious children will mature into globally conscious adults who are responsible, empathetic, enlightened citizens.

"Critical pedagogy is constructed on the belief that education is inherently political" (Kincheloe, 2008, p. 8). Every decision and action teachers engage in within the educational setting carries political connotation. From the books they choose to read, to the tests their students take, to even which students they group together for cooperative learning activities, these are all political decisions. "They refer to power and how it is distributed and engaged in the world of education and life in school" (Kincheloe, 2008, p. 8). Critical pedagogy offers teachers a framework to conceptualize power relations, how they affect their students, and ways in which they can mitigate these effects.

Education is not neutral. One example of politics in schools can be illustrated through prescribed curricula. Districts often adopt specific programs to align with state and/or federally mandated standards of learning, the given curriculum identifies facts and ideas to be studied. Alternative ways of thinking are not explored. School personnel may be under pressure from governmental bodies to construct or adopt a curriculum that is inflexible, unquestioning in its approach, and teacher-centered (Kincheloe, 2008, p. 9). As Kincheloe (2008) states, "Dominant power operates in numerous and often hidden ways" (p. 9). Many times, educators do not understand the underlying political implications of their daily work in schools. Critical pedagogy wants teachers to understand the political dynamics of education and how this insight can positively impact their students in terms of social justice and equity.

"Critical Pedagogy is dedicated to the alleviation of human suffering" (Kincheloe, 2008, p. 11). Critical pedagogy is foundationally concerned with mitigation of human anguish and oppression. Further, proponents of this pedagogy believe such suffering is a humanly constructed phenomenon and does not have to exist (Kincheloe, 2008, p. 11). Connecting students to other people through affective and emotional aspects of everyday life are of great concern to critical educators. Loving and caring for the world and the fellow man cannot be insincere or frivolous. Genuine love and care require dedication to the cause at hand. "Because love is an act of courage, not of fear, love is commitment to others. No matter where the oppressed are found, the act of love is commitment to their cause—the cause of liberation" (Freire, 2010, p. 89). Critical educators devote themselves to the people and the world in efforts to rectify social injustice. Cultivating authentic relationships is a significant ideology of critical pedagogy. Shields (2013) indicates that developing relationships facilitates learning. It is these relationships, and not prescribed programs, which become essential to successful teaching and learning and the promotion of private and ultimately public good (pp. 74–75). Sincere love and care in relationships with others are advantageous for the critical educator insofar as they assist in facilitating the progression of the social justice movement.

Kincheloe (2008) explains that critical pedagogy is a "Pedagogy that prevents students from being hurt" (p. 13). In our current era of educational accountability, fingers are pointed in every direction as to whom is responsible for the failures of public schools. Arguably, the most tragic victims are our students. They are frequently blamed for not learning and not achieving. Critical pedagogy means working in solidarity with marginalized populations as student voice work is committed to liberation. This type of educator must eliminate deficit thinking and blaming of the victim (Shields, 2013, p. 38). Authentic solidarity begins with mutual trust. It is essential that educators build a clear understanding of trust among those with whom they work and prove that their actions are consistent with their words. Freire (2010) articulates, "trusting the people is the indispensable precondition for revolutionary change. A real humanist can be identified more by his trust in the people, which engages them in their struggle, than by a thousand actions in their favor without trust" (p. 60). These actions often come in the form of false generosity; contributions and donations in the name of charity validate dominant power. The "handouts" to marginalized populations do not reflect the powerful as saviors they are merely a means of continued oppression. As Freire (2010) emphasizes, "salvation can be achieved only with others" (p. 146). Hence, solidarity is a cornerstone of democracy for critical pedagogy.

Critical educators work diligently to understand their students, meet them where they are at, and help them grow. Often, teachers are discouraged from taking into account their students' social, cultural, and economic backgrounds and their associated interests and needs (Kincheloe, 2008, p. 14). For the critical educator, environmental factors must be considered when measuring any kind of academic achievement. Furthermore, involving students in the educative process as valuable assets can combat some of the ways in which students are hurt in school.

Kincheloe's (2008) fifth characteristic of critical pedagogy is, "The importance of generative themes" (p. 15). Freire's notion of generative themes to read the word and the world gave students the opportunity to connect what they read on a page to the world around them. This, along with problem-posing education redefines what literacy means in the classroom. Critical educators promote students as researchers who critically analyze the world around them, ask difficult questions, and seek answers and solutions. "Critical students and teachers ask in the spirit of Freire and Horton: "please support us in our explorations of the world" (Kincheloe, 2008, p. 17). Power and traditional roles are challenged when the teacher no longer is the keeper of knowledge but a facilitator of learning.

Critical pedagogy views "teachers as researchers" (Kincheloe, 2008, p. 17). This idea empowers teachers to examine every aspect of schooling and researching their own practice. This can be achieved through thoughtful reflection. As Freire (2010) explains, "People will be truly critical...if their action encompasses a critical reflection which increasingly organizes their thinking and thus leads them to move from a purely naïve knowledge of reality to a higher level, one which enables them to perceive the causes of their reality" (p. 131). There are three essential types of reflection; reflection upon imposed programs, rules and regulations, self-reflection, and student reflection. The first area of reflection involves the constraints and limitations. This is particularly obvious in educational settings where teachers and administrators rely on prescribed programs and curricula that have been successful with specific students in very different settings. Reflection upon such programs helps educators realize that one size does not fit all; they understand the needs, strengths and deficits of the populations of students they serve and use that information as a basis for teaching and educating. Another area of reflection for leaders in the educational setting is that of state and federal mandates, most recently in the United States these constraints come in the form of universal standards and testing requirements. Because these policies are often linked to funds for schools, educators implement the programs without a second thought. Reflecting upon such programs and asking, "Is this educationally valuable for the children in my school?" would allow teachers and administrators to realize that these imposed programs are often too general to meet the needs of all children and should be modified or disregarded altogether. Critically informed educators are reflective upon such mandates in an effort to create more effective and positive environments.

The second area of reflection is that of self-reflection; this is a prerequisite for critical educators. Self-reflection requires humility; the admission that you can be wrong. Only when self-reflection is taken seriously is there room for growth. Reflection is an integral part of the learning process. It not only allows teachers to learn more about themselves and how they learn, but it also aids in improving skills. The third type of reflection is that of educating others on how to be self-reflective, particularly students. This is often an area overlooked by educators. However, if the goal of education is truly learning and understanding, self-reflection is a vital component. Although it can be a demanding practice to teach to children, without reflection it is almost impossible for true learning to occur. With huge demands to get through as much content as possible to prepare for state and federal tests, teachers often do not take the valuable time to teach students how to reflect on their work. Teachers often blame students for forgetting material they should have learned the year before, but in actuality, they likely never really learned it at all. Reflection is essential to move knowledge from short-term to long-term memory (Clements, n.d.). All three areas of reflection are imperative to critical educators. They understand that, "We don't learn from experience. We learn from reflecting on experience" (Dewey as cited in Clements, n.d.). These educators are advocates of education and learning. They are constantly searching for ways to improve themselves and those with whom they are working. The critical educator never achieves self-actualization for there is always room to further grow and develop the many facets of the self.

Kincheloe (2008) explains that "teachers as researchers of their students" is the seventh central characteristic of critical pedagogy (p. 19). Teachers need to engage in constant dialogue with their students and listen carefully to what students have to say regarding their communities and the issues that affect them (Kincheloe, 2008, p. 19). Student voice work is unquestioningly tied to ideas of empowerment, the goal of which is positive social action. Critical pedagogy attests that action cannot be entered into lightly or without the proper preparation. Most importantly, the critical educator must work in solidarity with marginalized populations for action to take place. There can be no action without the people for which the action is taking place. Freire (2010) further

INTRODUCTION 11

explains, a prerequisite of revolutionary action as dialogue. In dialogue, there are two components; reflection and action. Both must work in synchronization for transformation to occur. One cannot be sacrificed for the other; without action, there is only verbalism and without reflection, action becomes activism (p. 86). Only true action can yield real change.

Critical educators are responsive to the needs to of the populations with which they are working. They take time to meaningfully engage; they do not allow stereotypes to perpetuate their thinking and involvement with different groups. Educators do not have hidden agendas; their participation is strictly based on the needs of the people. They are not only receptive to the desires of the group but require them as an initial step in the process of reformation. It is necessary that they truly listen to the people and engage in meaningful dialogue. Freire (2010) discusses this dialogue at length, "founding itself upon love, humility, and faith, dialogue becomes a horizontal relationship of which mutual trust between the dialoguers is the logical consequence" (91). Free and open communication between all is essential to the success of the critical educator in his/her quest for equity. All topics of conversation should be accepted by the group and open for discussion unless they are harmful or perpetuate oppression. Individuals should feel a sense of hope and safety, free from judgment. This dialogue is essential to student voice work and provides educators with a means to understand and respond to the needs of the population.

Critical pedagogy is about "Social change and cultivating the intellect" (Kincheloe, 2008, p. 21). Critical teachers must work to understand the cultural differences of their students such as race, gender, ethnicity, socioeconomic class, religious beliefs, etc. Beyond a knowledge of their students' diversity, critical educators understand the ways in which these differences affect their students' achievement in school. "Without such an understanding, cultural and cognitive *difference* are confused with academic *deficiency*" (Kincheloe, 2008, p. 22). Critical teachers acknowledge the complexity of their students and the educational system. They view their practice as one that promotes positive social change and cultivates their students' intellect as well as their own.

Student voice work has a strong commitment to collaboration and one way in which educators can use critical pedagogical design in schools is through the establishment of democratic environments. They cannot be authoritarian in their leadership of the people; there is no room for condescending, false generosity or blaming. Inclusive, deeply democratic communities stem from educators engaging others in difficult conversations, modeling, teaching and presenting issues, topics and questions for consideration. These ideas should be open for dialogue in a nonthreatening environment, which is what I hope to have accomplished in my student interviews. In schools "teacher and students together comment, question, challenge one another, as they explore a topic from multiple angles, each bringing his or her insights to the communal learning, and in the process being enriched and enriching the understanding of others" (Shields, 2013, p. 43). Freire (2010) further examines this idea in his discussion of the banking concept, where the teacher possesses all of the knowledge and offers it to the students. In this example, the teacher is the authority and the students are subordinates. This is not a democratic environment. However, Freire (2010) explains that the critical transformative educator's efforts coincide with those of the students to engage in critical thinking and the quest for mutual humanization. The educator emanates a profound trust in people and their creative power. The teacher and student develop a strong partnership (p. 75). In this way Freire's educational system becomes a democracy. Learning from and working in solidarity with one another is at the heart of democracy. All perspectives and experiences are welcome and encouraged.

"Marginalization and critical pedagogy" is Kincheloe's (2008) ninth characteristic (p. 23). Critical pedagogy is concerned with those on the margins of society, those who are faced with oppression. Freire (2010) contends that social change cannot transpire without solidarity, trust, and dialogue. Leaders cannot persuade those they are assisting in liberation with propaganda or false generosity. "The conviction of the oppressed that they must fight for their liberation is not a gift bestowed by the revolutionary leadership, but the result of their own conscientização" (p. 67). Coming to a state of critical consciousness will guide and support the people on their journey out of oppression; this will also develop a need to free not only themselves but also those who are participating in the oppressing. It is important for critical educators to be sensitive to the enlightenment of the populations with which they are working; they cannot be an authority figure who thinks that they know what is best. This must be an organic process, for which time will need to be invested; however, success is inevitable when the oppressed truly liberate themselves.

In the educational setting, "critical teachers seek out individuals, voices, texts, and perspectives that had been previously excluded" (Kincheloe, 2008, p. 24). Mainstream education perpetuates the status-quo by excluding the knowledge of diverse populations. Critical teachers appreciate the cultural differences and dynamics of their classrooms and provide a safe place where students are enabled and encouraged to celebrate who they are. All forms of knowledge need to be part of the classroom experience for all students. When we focus on so-called typical knowledge we are promoting the oppression of our marginalized students.

Kincheloe (2008) recognizes "The importance of positivism" as his tenth characteristic of critical pedagogy (p. 28). Positivism contends that knowledge is produced in the physical sciences and social sciences in exactly the same ways. In this way, positivist behavioral and social scientists remove people from their cultural settings and study them in sterile conditions. Critical pedagogy argues that humans cannot be understood outside of the context that formed them (Kincheloe, 2008). Within this positivist view, everyone is viewed as the same and universal applications are appropriate and necessary. This is important for the critical teacher to understand, particularly as common learning standards are mandated, standardized tests are used to measure student achievement and growth, and prescribed and scripted curricula are adopted.

Echoing positivism, Kincheloe (2008) identifies "The force of science to regulate" as his eleventh central characteristic of critical pedagogy (p. 30). He points out that critical educators question and critique science as there is always more than what can be seen on the surface. There is more than one way to view the world and critical pedagogy recognizes the importance of multiple perspectives (Kincheloe, 2008). The ways that science is studied in school, is regulatory in nature. The historical narratives of our textbooks recount powerful Western culture and scarce views of others. There is little room given to critique of scientific knowledge as presented in the educational setting. These approaches to science regulate what an 'acceptable' view of the world is, while excluding all others.

Finally, Kincheloe (2008) explains that critical pedagogy is "cognizant of the importance of understanding the context in which the educational activity takes place" (p. 31). In the daily milieu of standardization and accountability, this can be especially difficult for educators to embody. Critical pedagogy requires educators to examine the relationships and contexts connecting culture, learner, curriculum, and knowledge production. Learning is viewed as complex and uncertain. There is no room for universal applications in this dynamic environment. Understanding these contextual factors assist educators in facilitating the needs of their students. "Context may be more important than content" (Kincheloe, 2008, p. 33). Critical teachers do not view problems, data, curriculum, culture, and knowledge in isolation. These factors can only be understood when taking into account the context in which they occur.

I believe critical pedagogy is an important foundation for educators and for my work. "Critical theory is grounded in a social view of justice and promotes a fundamental rethinking and reconceptualization of school-related issues" (Gorlewski, 2012, p. 239). It is important for students and teachers to examine current power structures as related to standardization and assessment. Unpacking these problems helps us understand them more deeply and theorize ways in which we can positively impact our education system. At the school level, critical pedagogy as basis for student voice work "is expressed in specific projects which explicitly articulate the connection between student voice practice and he notion of empowerment" (Taylor & Robinson, 2009, p. 165). An understanding of Kincheloe's characteristics of critical pedagogy directly supports the theoretical framework of my research.

CHAPTER 2

Understanding High-Stakes Standardized Exams in the US

> *The bureaucratic and technical approach to schools—establish content, prescribe content, and measure student acquisition of that content—has been visited and revisited decade after decade for more than a century now. It has always failed and it always will.*
> THOMAS (2012, p. 56)

∴

The History

While standardized assessment has long been present in United States education, the high-stakes nature of such tests is a more recent phenomenon. Leistyna (2007) explains that the roots of this assessment trend can be traced to two compelling events, the 1957 Soviet Union launch of Sputnik that questioned the intellectual capabilities of the youth of the United States; and the release of The Coleman Report in 1966, which "initiated a major shift in national strategy from targeting resources and their impact on student achievement to a focus on measuring individual performance" (p. 61). The Coleman Report was conducted only one year after the passage of President Lyndon B. Johnson's Elementary and Secondary Education Act (ESEA). Not only had insufficient time elapsed between the enactment of the legislation and the study conducted, the report clearly outlined the inequalities of racial segregation in public schools, which contradicted the reported findings that ESEA was fighting poverty (Schneider, 2015).

ESEA was enacted as part of the Johnson Administration's War on Poverty campaign. "The law's original goal, which remains today, was to improve educational equity for students from lower income families by providing funds to school districts serving poor students" (Atlas, 2015, p. 1). This legislation was a foundational step toward the federal government's involvement in offering designated funds to states as opposed to general financial assistance (Schneider, 2015). ESEA has been reauthorized seven times since its debut (1972,

1978, 1983, 1989, 1994, 2001, and 2015). As we are chiefly concerned with the standardized assessment apportionment, attention will be focused upon the two most recent reauthorizations. Before exploring those, the 1983 National Commission on Education report, *A Nation at Risk* is worth noting. In this study, it was argued that schools in the United States were performing poorly in comparison to other industrialized countries and the United States was in jeopardy of losing its global superiority. Although high-stakes tests existed in some states, they had not been deemed productive reforms, nor had they warranted the expansion of high-stakes testing policies. Nevertheless, to alleviate the situation, *A Nation at Risk* called for standards and tests to improve the academic achievement of America's youth. The commission recommended that states establish higher standards and administer assessments to hold schools accountable for meeting those standards. These assessments became known as high-stakes tests (Amrein & Berliner, 2002).

Now, to revisit the ESEA reauthorizations of 2001 and 2015. Perhaps the most infamous education legislation ever enacted was the passage of the 2001 reauthorization of ESEA, named No Child Left Behind (NCLB). George Bush's NCLB "became the first national framework linking standards, assessment, and accountability" (Smith, 2014, p. 9). Schools were to be evaluated on their ability to make Annual Yearly Progress (AYP) through the use of student scores on standardized tests. Those schools that did not meet AYP for three years in a row were subject to deep sanctions, restructuring, and further reform efforts. This law also included the insurmountable requirement that *all* students score proficient in reading and math as measured by standardized tests by 2014 (Schneider, 2015). To this end, NCLB required states to develop timelines outlining how 100% of their students would reach proficiency in math and reading by 2013–2014 (Ravitch, 2016, p. 103).

As this 2014 date loomed near and NCLB failed to produce overall test score gains or close racial gaps, a new initiative was offered, which pushed for national, common standards. In 2009, the Common Core initiative, which is a set of math and English/Language Arts standards and aligned standardized tests, had been adopted fully by 46 states and three US territories through US Secretary of Education Arne Duncan's Race to the Top (RTTP).

> More than $4 billion of this money has been reserved for the competitive Race to the Top grants, which present the nation's governors with an extraordinary opportunity to make bold reforms in education. In a budget year when most states are struggling just to keep education funding stable, the Race to the Top funds provide governors who are ready to push for innovative education reform with much-needed funding. (Schneider, 2015, p. 165)

States, like mine, found themselves with no choice other than to commit to the criteria stipulated by the RTTT competition: Common Core State Standards (CCSS) and corresponding assessments developed and administered by one of two approved consortia among other obligations (Schneider, 2015, p. 164).

NCLB Section 1111 under Subpart 1—Basic Program Requirements outlines State Plans for any State desiring to receive grants through NCLB. One portion of this section details academic assessments. In brief, States must

1. implement a set of high-quality, yearly student academic assessments that include math, reading/language arts, and science,
2. use the same academic assessments to measure the achievement of all children,
3. align assessments to academic achievement standards,
4. test students in grades three through eight,
5. include measures that assess higher-order thinking skills and understanding (US Department of Education, 2005, pp. 5–6).

These noted requirements commonly speak to the federal condition that States must implement a standardized assessment to all students in public schools. The two multi-state consortia; the Smarter Balanced Assessment Consortium (SBAC) and the Partnership for Assessment of Readiness for College and Careers (PARCC), won federal grants (respectively, $160 million and $170 million federal startup grants) to develop Common Core tests that meet this requirement. As will be discussed later, my state chose the Pearson developed PARCC test for our students.

Fast-forward to the current 2015 reauthorization of ESEA. President Obama's administration renamed this law the Every Student Succeeds Act (ESSA), which was rewritten eight years late (Strauss, 2015). The Executive Office of the President (2015) claimed that this legislation would ensure states set high standards, maintain accountability, empower state and local decision-makers, preserve annual assessments and reduce the often onerous burden of unnecessary and ineffective testing, provide more children access to high-quality preschool, and establish new resources. However, many critics agree with Karp's (2016) sentiment that ESSA is merely NCLB repackaged, which is evidenced by the familiar components outlined by the Executive Office of the President. Let's unpack the provisions of assessment as they are delineated in the ESSA legislation.

Assessment in America: ESSA
The Every Student Succeeds Act (2015) states:

> Each State plan shall demonstrate that the State educational agency... has implemented a set of high-quality student academic assessments

in mathematics, reading or language arts, and science...the assessments shall...be the *same academic assessments used to measure the achievement of all public elementary school and secondary school students* in the state and administered to all public elementary school and secondary school students in the state and *be aligned with the challenging State academic standards,* and provide coherent and timely information about student attainment of such standards and whether the student is performing at the student's grade level; be used for which such assessments are valid and reliable, consistent, with *relevant nationally recognized professional and technical testing standards,* objectively measure academic achievement, knowledge, and skills, and be tests that do not evaluate or assess personal or family beliefs and attitudes or publically disclose personally identifiable information...in the case of mathematics and reading or language arts be administered in each of grades 3 through 8 and at least once in grades 9 through 12; in the case of science not less than one time during grades 3 through 5; grades 6 through 9; and grades 10 through 12...*involve multiple up-to-date measures of student academic achievement,* including measures that assess higher-order thinking skills and understanding, which may include measures of academic growth and may be partially delivered *in the form of portfolios, projects, or extended performance tasks.* (S1177-24–S1177-25, emphasis added)

There remain many other stipulations regarding assessments that further specify state requirements. However, I have chosen the most relevant for this discussion. I have emphasized a few portions of the above text to note (1) not much has changed with regard to assessment from NCLB to this ESSA legislation, the requirement that students in public education take a total of 17 tests in their 10 years of schooling remains (2) as do the standards, many states have recently begun full implementation of the CCSS it is unlikely states, like mine, will eliminate them and develop new standards. (3) Notice the phrasing of, *relevant nationally recognized professional and technical testing standards;* these federally approved testing conglomerates cost states millions of dollars, as is the case with Pearson my state. (4) Finally, the sentence regarding alternative-type assessments to the standardized testing obligation is both convoluted and contradictory. It is as if the legislatures responsible for drafting this law wanted to assure state educators that they may (superficially) use their own (albeit much more beneficial) assessments to fulfill this requirement.

Senator David P. Cleary, chief of staff to Senator Lamar Alexander of Tennessee, who led the reauthorization of NCLB, explained that the federal testing requirement of NCLB was not a problem, it was the accountability system attached to it. He claims that "we decided [with ESSA] to focus on reducing the federally determined high stakes attached to the tests—creating an environment where states could reduce the extra tests they were administering and, most importantly, develop their own accountability system to judge whether schools and teachers were succeeding in educating students" (Ravitch, 2016). While this is in fact what the legislation states, as one would predict it is much more complicated than that. There is the illusion that this federal legislation bestows more power to the states involving standardized assessment, that is clearly not the case when one examines the later section 1111(c)(4)(E) of ESSA (2015):

> Annually measure the achievement of not less than 95 percent of all students, and 95 percent of all students in each subgroup of students, who are enrolled in public schools on the assessments...provide a clear and understandable explanation of how the State will factor this requirement of clause of this subparagraph into the statewide accountability system. (S.1177-36)

Schneider (2016) points out that ESSA requires 95 percent of enrolled students complete the mandated tests and also includes a disclaimer that states cannot hang any opt-out laws on ESSA's Title I testing mandate. What this does is pit schools and districts against states regarding these ESSA Title I tests. As a result, the federal government demands that states make 95 percent of students take the tests (and simultaneously remove themselves from any opt-out responsibilities) so that the states must pressure schools and districts to administer them (Schneider, 2016). In this way, nothing has changed in terms of required tests, opting out, and NCLB.

Noticeably absent from all of this legislation are student voices. Cook-Sather (2006) elaborates,

> This elision is consistent with the tendency for educational research to be conducted *on* not *with* students. It is also consistent with the tendency of both the educational system in the United States and that system's every reform to focus exclusively on adults' notions of how education should be conceptualized and practiced. (p. 372)

The blatant lack of value placed upon students as capable participants in matters that affect them is precisely the rationale for my research. I vehemently believe that children are intelligent contributors who have important thoughts and opinions about schooling.

In an effort to fulfill the specifications as devised by the federal NCLB policy, states across the country enacted new education legislation. The Midwestern state where I work and conducted my research created and decreed Senate Bill 3412. This state law delineates the ways in which the state will meet the assessment requirements. In brief, (1) beginning in the 2014–2015 the State Board of Education will annually assess students in grades three through twelve in English/Language Arts (ELA) and Mathematics, (2) Students will be assessed in Science beginning in the 2017–2018 school year, (3) Students at the secondary level who are not assessed for college and career determinations may not receive a high school diploma, (4) student scores on these college and career ready assessments must be placed in the student's permanent record, and (5) these assessments must consist of questions and answers that are measurable and quantifiable to measure the knowledge, skills, and ability of students (State General Assembly, n.d., pp. 6–9). On June 18, 2014, the State Board of Education authorized the State Superintendent to enter into a four-year contract with NCS Pearson, Inc., for $160,503,958 for the purpose of developing, administering, scoring, and reporting the PARCC summative assessment aligned to the CCSS in ELA and mathematics (ISBE, 2014, p. 253).

As this state law, like many others across the country, began permeating local school systems, districts throughout the state created their own assessment policies in response. Despite the Pearson contract's recent expiration, the state has chosen to continue its partnership with PARCC. In a letter to school superintendents, the State Superintendent of Education writes, "Illinois will continue to use and build on the core features of PARCC that make it the highest quality accountability assessment available in the United States" (Smith, 2018). Alliances, like these, between governing bodies and large corporations along with the newly enacted ESSA legislation guarantee that high-stakes exams will persist in public education in the foreseeable future.

Pearson

Pearson is an international education powerhouse. Their history began as a construction company in 1844 and transformed into an acquisition company focused on publishing, international media, and education (Schneider, 2015, pp. 176–177). Most recently, over the past 20 years, Pearson Learning has become the dominant publisher of educational textbooks and education-related materials used throughout P-12 public education and in higher education in the US (Attick & Boyles, 2016, p. 5). Pearson penetrates every aspect of education. As Apple (2014) contends, "by and large Pearson will become the department of education in the United States, and in many ways that's happening now" (as cited in Attick & Boyles, 2016, p. 6). Pearson's power has largely been established by their political connections, lobbying, and influence over state and federal education policy (Attick & Boyles, 2016, p. 6).

Gutstein (2012) discusses Pearson's "three-pronged" approach to controlling the education market. First, Pearson uses its huge profits to aggressively acquire competitors. Between 2007–2013 they spent five billion dollars to buy 25 education publishing companies. Second, Pearson intends to dominate online content delivery through their development of courses that promote choice and flexibility. Third, Pearson's role in standardizing teacher education certification through the Education Teacher Performance Assessment (edTPA) and their "customizable" online learning modules promotes Pearson's notion of personalized education (as cited in Attick & Boyles, 2016, pp. 6–7). Diane Ravitch (2012) refers to the ever-increasing prevalence of Pearson as "The Pearsonizing of the American Mind." Infiltrating every facet of American education, Pearson continues to partner and purchase various educational companies and groups to ensure their stronghold.

The edTPA has provided Pearson with its best access yet to the teacher education market. EdTPA was developed at the Stanford Center for Assessment, Learning, and Equity (SCALE) with the American Association of Colleges of Teacher Education (AACTE). EdTPA attempts to increase accountability for teacher education programs and candidates (Attick & Boyles, 2016, p. 9). As Tuck and Gorlewski (2016) explain, "edTPA represents the normalization of teaching as a technical and apolitical act, of examinations as meaningful measures of complex acts and useful instruments for surveillance and discipline, and of relationships and local contexts as subordinate to distant, objective expertise" (p. 203). The edTPA is merely the newest controlling mechanism enacted through the heavy-hand of corporate driven policy reminiscent of the CCSS and PARCC. Edtpa.aacte.org (n.d.) reports that currently there are 734 Educator Preparation Programs in 38 states and the District of Columbia participating in edTPA. Twelve states (including this Midwestern state) already have formally adopted edTPA for statewide use to license new teachers or approve teacher preparation programs.

Pearson also gains leverage to impact policy through their "charitable" donations. Schneider (2015) reports that in 2009, Pearson Charitable Foundation paid over half a million dollars to one of the two organizations that holds the license for the Common Core State Standards (CCSS) (p. 178). As public schools across the country were forced into adoption of the CCSS they needed aligned materials and of course, federally-approved assessments. As one of two CCSS assessment consortia, the Partnership for Assessment of Readiness for College and Careers (PARCC) awarded Pearson the contract ($240 million per year) to develop the PARCC test despite their well-established history of testing errors (Schneider, 2015, pp. 180–188).

Bob Schaeffer, public education director of FairTest: National Center for Fair and Open Testing, has kept a log of the company's quality-control problems. Over the past twenty years, he cites 72 incidences worldwide in Pearson's History of Testing Problems (2018). And surely, we can recall, Pearson's story of *The Hare and the Pineapple*, which was an eighth-grade comprehension passage with corresponding multiple-choice questions (Pinkwater, n.d.). The story is practically incomprehensible and the questions even more absurd. Asking students "Which animal spoke the wisest words?" And the correct response was "The Owl," which was never even mentioned in the passage (Rotherham, 2012). Despite a well-documented record of errors and issues, Pearson's influence continues to expand and intensify.

Consequences

Standardization and subsequent high-stakes testing persist in our educational systems for a variety of reasons; from corporate interest, reinforcing the status quo, privatizing schools, or simply control. Despite resistance from public groups these measures are becoming more influential and obtrusive in students' everyday lives.

The implementation of universal standards themselves imply (1) that teachers do not know how to educate students in an adequate way to meet the needs of the political agenda and (2) that all children should be the same. While all of those involved in the education process are affected in some way or another by standardized assessment the two groups I will focus on are teachers and students in an effort to rationalize my work.

Teachers
Perhaps the most demoralizing aspect of the standardization movement is the deprofessionalization of teachers. Scripted, narrow curriculum is regularly mandated for teachers to implement in their classrooms. Movements such as these essentially strip teachers of their competence and autonomy.

Tests are continuously shaping what is taught in schools. When teachers teach to the test, the exams define the curriculum. As teachers become familiar with the PARCC test they analyze the requirements, see the test questions themselves, and use what they learn in an effort to give their students an advantage on the test. By doing so, teachers teach students how to respond to practice test items even if they never learn the underlying concepts (Amrein & Berliner,

2002, p. 40). In Jones and Egley's 2007 study of teachers' perceptions regarding test-based accountability programming, they found that teachers were spending an average of 43.0% of their mathematics instructional time, 42.6% of their writing instructional time, and 38.0% of their reading instructional time on test-taking strategies (p. 241). This is an enormous amount of time, that could have been used in more thoughtful educative ways had the pressures of standardized testing not been influencing. Further, Jones and Engley (2007) cite a teacher describing how teaching to the test is not the same as 'real learning,'

> Schools aren't improving their academics as students score better on the test. They are just taking more time to teach to the test and, unfortunately, away from real learning. We aren't getting smarter students; we are getting smarter test takers. That is NOT what we are here for! The schools that score well are focusing on teaching to test at a very high cost to their students. (p. 241)

When educators feel the need to teach to the test, frequently they are both teaching irrelevant information and many of the concepts and skills necessary for such exams are developmentally inappropriate. All of these ideas narrow the curriculum and deskill both teachers and students.

High-stakes tests are directing what subject and content areas are being taught in schools. Math and language arts are most frequently tested and therefore all other subject matter is being overlooked. Schaeffer, Neill, and Guisbond (2012) report, "that test-driven schooling damaged educational quality and equity by narrowing curriculum and focusing on the limited skills that standardized tests measure" (p. 38). This sentiment is echoed over and over again in the research of standardized testing, yet we are continuously moving in the direction of increased universality and accountability of our schools and curriculum.

Further, Minarechova (2012) explains, "teachers often leave the teaching profession because of what is going on under the name "accountability" and "tougher standards" (p. 95). The pressures placed upon educators to view their students as numbers in a data set and to raise those numbers by any means necessary is more than disconcerting. True educators get into the field to teach, to make a difference in the lives of young people, and contribute to a passion for learning among other benevolent reasons; not to perpetuate the status quo or corporate agenda.

Students

Naturally, the consequences for teachers affect students. To begin, when standardized tests become the central focus of education students are not only subjected to narrow curriculum they must also suffer through developmentally inappropriate and irrelevant content all in the name of increased test scores. Standardized tests do not consider children's developmental rates, many tasks that students are required to perform are inappropriate for their intellectual maturity. Unfortunately, this means that educators are teaching their students to jump through the hoops to pass the test, but true understanding is not happening. For example, I was required to teach my third graders comparing and ordering fractions so that they were prepared for the PARCC test in the spring, but they never really understood that a fraction is less than one. This is just one small example of how teaching advanced skills to students who are not developmentally prepared is utterly unsuccessful and demotivating for both the teacher and the students.

Educational scholars have long cited the importance of relevant content, which is why it is so disconcerting to recognize the extent to which irrelevant information is being taught in schools today. This is chiefly due to the influence of standardized tests. Along these lines, in their study of Chinese English Language Learners, Xiao and Carless (2013) found that students were able to complete and pass tests about the English language and its usage but were unable to use and understand the language in real-life (p. 329). This conclusion exemplifies the importance of content. Students are learning more and more about nothing. Educators teach what is on the test in isolation and without any effort to connect the material to students' lives, which means actual understanding and future application is impossible.

Other consequences of high-stakes testing are grade retention and expulsion. Some researchers posit that low-achieving students are being retained in grades the year before pivotal testing years in states with high school graduation exams so students can have more time to prepare for high-stakes tests. This may also be practiced so the scores of low-performing students will not negatively skew classroom, school, and district composite scores (Amrein & Berliner, 2002, p. 35). Further, some students (especially at the high-school level) are being expelled before, or dismissed from school during, the administration of high-stakes tests. This develops because these students' potentially low test scores will impact school or district averages (Minarechova, 2012, p. 89).

Undoubtedly, there are countless consequences of standardized tests affecting the many stakeholders in public education. To name a few more (1) financial consequence; there is great money to be made in the standards movement: money for publishers of tests and materials, for charter school owners, for inventors of teacher evaluation programs, for computer and software companies, (2) political consequence; there is political advantage for business people and politicians in these hard economic times to demonize teachers, their unions, and other public sector employees (Jolley, 2014, p. 82), and (3) cheating; investigations increasingly find that administrators, teachers, and students are cheating on these exams for a variety of reasons, all which stem from the national pressure and accountability measures through assessment policy (Minarechova, 2012, p. 94).

CHAPTER 3

What Is Student Voice?

> *We acknowledge that if students are provided with opportunities to think, share, communicate, and make the cognitive connections necessary for understanding, we are able to transform them from passive to active participants in their education and, ultimately, create a population eager and interested in learning every day of their lives.*
>
> MILLHAM (2012, P. 181)

∴

Context

"Student voice is a normative project and has its basis in an ethical and moral practice which aims to give students the right of democratic participation in school processes (Taylor & Robinson, 2009, p. 161). With admirable and meaningful foundations, student voice work takes great effort and caution to maintain its purpose beyond superficiality. In the early 1990's a number of educators and social critics noticed the exclusion of student voices from conversations about learning, teaching, and schooling. Scholars from the United States, like Kozol and Weis and Fine along with others around the world, began the conversation to rethink this exclusion and began the calling for student voice in education (Cook-Sather, 2006, pp. 361–362). The developing discourse produced a "new vocabulary" with terms like opinion, matter, capable, listen actively, and involve.

As the discussion regarding student voice began to change so did the field itself. Cook-Sather (2006) explains that in the late 1990's and early 2000's,

> Many of the educational research and reform efforts that have unfolded in Australia, Canada, England, and the United States that encourage reflection, discussion, dialogue and action on matters that primarily concern students, but also, by implication, school staff and the communities they serve have been encompassed by the term "student voice". (p. 362)

There began an educational shift to hear the voices of students; legitimizing their opinions and perspectives in an effort for them to be actively involved in their education.

McIntyre, Pedder, and Rudduck (2005) argue that schools cannot claim their primary purpose is to benefit students if the students' own views about what is beneficial to them are not actively sought and attended to (p. 150). Students have a great deal to offer the educational community for which they are an integral part. There can be found instances of triumphant accomplishment and frivolous application in the brief twenty-five-year history of student voice in educational research and practice.

In Research

Waxman and Huang (1997) ascertain that understanding how students perceive and react to their learning environments is likely more effective than the analysis of outsiders (p. 40). Similarly, Howard (2001) reports, "that researchers analyze student perspectives of classroom instruction and learning environments since what students experience in learning may be quite different from observed or intended pedagogy" (p. 133). There are countless instances where adults; teachers, parents, and administrators, are consulted regarding what is best for education, when students who are most involved, arguably the most important stakeholders, are notably absent in the literature.

Lodge (2005) suggests that student voice can be investigated in two ways: the role of the student and the purposes for student participation. She identifies four types:
1. Quality control: The purpose is to listen to students simply as sources of feedback on externally imposed approaches to school improvement.
2. Students as a source of information: Student perspectives are listened to and then improvement is done to them or students provide information for teachers to act upon.
3. Compliance and control: Takes some account of ideas about the rights of students to be included in decisions about school yet the students' voice is utilized to serve institutional ends.
4. Dialogue: Students are seen as active participants and their voices are included as part of ongoing discourse (as cited in Cook-Sather, 2006, p. 377).

These approaches illustrate the spectrum for which educational institutions employ the practice of student voice. Types 1–3 are the most common ways student input is collected in schools. For example, members of student councils participate in school board meetings with members and administration to represent the voice of the student body. While the group will most likely listen to the student representatives, their thoughts and ideas are not valued unless they align with the ideologies of the established membership. The aim of my work is to promote student voice as a dialogue. While I queried the student interviewees with questions about their experiences with the PARCC test, I worked to engage them in conversation. I intended to be very clear about the importance of this research and the reasons why I chose to interview students. Their underrepresented and critical voice needs to be heard, especially with regard to the prevalence of standardization and high-stakes accountability.

Similar to Lodge's work, Fielding (2001) establishes levels of student involvement in school self-review and school improvement through the Students as Researchers (SAR) approach in the UK. Students as Researchers was an initiative where students themselves identified issues they perceived as substantial within their daily school experience and, with staff support, gathered and analyzed data, and developed recommendations for change to share with their peers, the staff, and the administration (Fielding, 2001, p. 125). Fielding (2001) suggests that it is essential to reflect upon what is meant by student voice and student involvement as well as whose purposes are served through utilization. He offers a four-fold model, which differentiates between students as sources of data, students as active respondents, students as co-researchers, and students as researchers (p. 135). Below I have extracted the most beneficial descriptors to the current discussion from each of Fielding's four categories:

1. Students as *Data Source*: Knowing about student performance and attitudes towards learning. Teachers interact with students by acknowledging.
2. Students as *Active Respondents:* Knowing how students learn. Teachers interact with students by hearing.
3. Students as *Co-Researchers*: Knowing what students might be able to contribute to deepen understanding. Teachers interact with students by listening in order to learn.
4. Students as *Researchers:* Knowing what teachers and peers might be able to contribute to deepen understanding. Teachers interact with students by listening in order to contribute (Fielding, 2001, p. 136).

It is my hope that this work contributes to the improvement of schools and public education, which is why Fielding's levels are pertinent here. In my research, the student participants are Active Respondents however; there are many characteristics of Students as Co-Researchers that correlate as well. For example, within Students as Active Respondents, the role of the student is a discussant, which applies to this work. Additionally, within Students as Co-Researchers meaning is made through teacher-led dialogue, which directly corresponds to my data analysis. As with any qualitative study using human subjects there is fluidity in categorization.

Research with student-voice focus tends to be conducted through qualitative studies in a semi-structured interview or focus group setting. For example, DeFur and Korinek (2010) conducted focus groups of middle and high-school students regarding their "perspectives on the nature of schools, teaching and administration that influence learning" (p. 15). McIntyre et al. (2005) interviewed Year 8 students regarding what they did and did not find helpful in their learning and in their teacher's teaching in general, as well as soliciting alternatives they thought would help them learn better (pp. 151–152). Additionally, Howard (2001) conducted individual interviews and a subsequent focus group with elementary-school students. The intentions of this methodology were two-fold (1) to "gain insight into viewpoints that are rarely revealed in the research about teaching ethnically and culturally diverse students" and (2) to understand the extent to which their viewpoints were consistent with those of both an outside observer and the teachers' intended goals (p. 136).

For students in higher education, student voice research methodology typically shifts from interviews to more quantitative measures. Iannone and Simpson (2013) administered a questionnaire to undergraduate mathematics students to investigate their perceptions of assessment methods (pp. 22 & 27). When the study participants are adults, namely teachers and administrators, both qualitative and quantitative methodologies are present. Cormack and Comber's (2013) qualitative study of the ways in which new high-stakes literacy tests are changing how educators teach and work in rural Australia was conducted through interviews and focus group discussions (pp. 78 & 82). On the other hand, Jones and Egley's (2007) quantitative study of intermediate teachers was conducted through an online survey to examine teachers' perceptions of how Florida's testing program had affected students' learning (pp. 235–236). As recently established, while educational studies regarding human perception can be organized in varied ways, I am committed to utilizing a qualitative approach because of the value I place upon student voice in my research.

In Practice

When exploring student voice as a school or classroom practice the literature reveals two distinctly noticeable yet overlapping divisions between (1) who is heard and (2) how educators listen. Power relations between and among students and educators influence both of these areas. Alcoff (2004) articulates this notion well,

>Whether acknowledged or not, issues of voice are embedded in historically located structures and relations of power. Who is speaking to whom turns out to be as important for meaning and truth as what is said; in fact what is said turns out to change according to who is speaking and who is listening. (as cited in Cook-Sather p. 363)

This is precisely why student voice as an ideology has a positive connotation yet can be utilized in superficial ways that render its existence arbitrary instead of empowering.

Who Is Heard

Classroom hierarchies are a well-documented phenomenon that contribute to the influence some students have over others when it comes to student voice in the educational setting. Those students with higher social capital become the voices that teachers tend to listen to, while those from marginalized groups based on race or class for example, are ignored. Reay's (2006) research of consulting primary school pupils about learning found that the creation of 'top sets' in the class with labels like 'gifted and talented' both encourage and exacerbate power dynamics inevitably silencing certain groups of pupils (p. 179). Likewise, Taylor and Robinson (2009) ascertain, "participation in student voice work becomes a 'dividing practice,' separating off the confident and articulate students from those pupils whose voices are silenced because they don't fit the dominant discourse and academic aspirations of their schools" (p. 168). Those who aspire to engage students in meaningful discourse must be cognizant of the dynamics of the classroom and the inevitable intentional or unintentional hierarchies among students. McIntyre et al. (2005) expand upon this notion of who is heard, "pupils differ in the confidence and articulateness with which they can express their ideas—and we know that such differences often reflect social class distinctions" (p. 155). This is yet another factor that influences both student voice research and the ways that students are listened to by their teachers. Finally, assuming that the aim of research is to assure all students have a voice, the cross-selection of participants must encompass children who may be more reserved in their responsiveness. With the provisions and protections in place for student participants in qualitative research, this would assuredly be a difficult endeavor. However, acknowledging the existence of which student voices are heard and how this is a contributing factor to the research, valuable information can nevertheless be obtained from such a study.

Another aspect in this realm is the superficiality of facilitating and using student voice. "The fact that student voice has most often been allied to agendas around school improvement means that in the 'present performance-dominated climate' student voice might be co-opted to produce 'surface compliance' rather than deeper modes of reflection and engagement (Taylor & Robinson, 2009, p. 163). Indeed, the illusion that students are participating in school reform efforts is well documented. For example, practically every middle school and high school across the country has a student government that is encouraged to participate in school improvement work yet their intentions must align to the dominant ideology to be accepted.

It is critical that those in power, whether that be as researchers or educators listen to children from all backgrounds to gain a fuller and more meaningful understanding of the student experience. "Listening to and dialoguing with all types of students—not just the high achievers or natural leaders—and encouraging them to voice their opinions promotes community, a sense of belonging, and increased student engagement" (DeFur & Korinek, 2010, p. 19). The differences in and among populations of students are inevitable. It becomes necessary to acknowledge and support all children in finding and using their voices for equitable change to come to fruition.

Teachers Listen

When the function of student voice work is one of engaging students to actively participate in their educational experience, it is necessary for teachers to listen to the perspectives and feedback their students convey. Students are no longer passive observers in the classroom; they become partners in the educative process. Cook-Sather (2006) explains,

> When students speak out on their own behalf, and when what they say matters—indeed, shapes action—student voice becomes the initiating force in an enquiry process which invites teachers' involvement as facilitating and enabling partners in learning rather than keeping students in the role of recipient or victim of teachers' decision-making process. (p. 366)

Again, this concept relates to power dynamics in the classroom. Asking a teacher to relinquish some of his/her control can be a difficult endeavor. Teachers must be open to the possibilities and value of student perspectives and suggestions.

McIntyre et al. (2005) explain that only when teachers believe that student perspectives are valuable and important will they make the sustained effort necessary to both engage in pupil consultation and to change their teaching in response (pp. 166–167). It is not merely enough to engage students in dialogue about educational issues; teachers must be open and prepared to genuinely listen to what students have to say.

> Sometimes I wish I could sit down with one of my teachers and just tell them what I exactly think about their class. It might be good, it might be bad, it's just that you don't have the opportunity to do it. (Cook-Sather, 2006, p. 376)

That is likely the most humbling aspect of student voice work; to hear what you may not want to know. Teachers often believe they are working in the best interest of their students and the potential to debunk that notion can be intimidating. However, as McIntyre et al. (2005) found in their research, students "seemed to value the opportunity to reflect and talk seriously about what helped them learn" (p. 152). Student voice as a philosophy needs to be engaged as a partnership where all participants can freely participate in dialogue as partners willing to learn from one another. I hope that my work contributes to this ideology.

CHAPTER 4

How Foucault's Governmentality Can Help

> *It is the examination which, by combining hierarchical surveillance and normalizing judgement, assures the great disciplinary functions of distribution and classification*
> FOUCAULT (1995, p. 192)

∴

The Theory

Michel Foucault's governmentality is a term that can be utilized and interpreted in varied ways dependent upon the circumstances. As with any social theory, the perceived benefits and shortcomings are analyzed through the specific lens of the researcher. To ground this research, I will explore the theory of governmentality through my personal context and experiences with elementary education, standardized assessment, and student voice practices. Through my research, I have encountered an extensive variety of ways in which scholars define Foucault's governmentality. However, one key element is commonly present, government as the conduct of conduct (Foucault, 1982, pp. 220–221). In this way, I will begin by discussing how conduct is shaped through Foucault's mechanisms of control.

Mechanisms of Control

In his 1975–76 Lectures at the Collège de France, Foucault (1997) establishes power's hold over life historically progressed from man as a body to man as a species and the birth of biopower (pp. 240–264). While forms of discipline and mechanisms of control between these disciplinary and regulatory periods are not mutually exclusive I have organized them in two separate, yet related subsections.

Disciplinary

Disciplinary mechanisms of control are characteristically individualizing and techniques of power are centered on the body. These structures of government emerged in the sixteenth to eighteenth centuries through secular formation

(Dean, 2010, p. 89). The notion that the state should care for the welfare of its citizens developed during this time as pastoral power. In this way, power is exerted as care through knowledge. Foucault personifies this type of control through the likeness of the shepherd and his flock.

Foucault (1981) establishes some critical themes typical of pastoral power in the Christian allegory of the shepherd and his flock. (1) "The shepherd wields power over a flock rather than over a land," (2) "the shepherd gathers together, guides, and leads his flock," (3) "The shepherd's role is to ensure the salvation of his flock," and (4) "wielding power is a 'duty'" (pp. 228–230). Additionally, (5) the shepherd must account for each of his sheep and their actions, (6) the flock complies to the will of the shepherd through pure obedience, and (7) the knowledge between the shepherd and each of his sheep is deeply particular (pp. 236–237). Next, I will frame the ideas represented by Foucault's metaphor in terms of governmental control. (1) The relationship between those in power and the governed citizens is of greatest importance, (2) the immediate presence and direct action of a governmental body is the primary cause society as a whole exists, (3) the welfare state ensures the wellbeing of its individual citizens, (4) a constant concern of the governing body is maintaining the good of the masses through surveillance and individual attention to each member, (5) power is held in the comprehensive understanding of each individual and his/her actions, (6) citizens depend on the government, which requires their obedience, and (7) the knowledge between the governing body and those governed is individualizing, as it is not enough to understand the state of society, specific knowledge of each member is necessary.

Disciplinary technologies of control, characteristic of pastoral power began shifting around the midpoint of the eighteenth century. Foucault (1997) explains,

> This [new] technology of power does not exclude the former, does not exclude disciplinary technology, but it does dovetail into it, integrate it, modify it to some extent, and above all, use it by sort of infiltrating it, embedding itself in existing disciplinary techniques…Unlike discipline, which is addressed to bodies, the new nondisciplinary power is applied not to man-as-body but to…man-as-species. (p. 243)

Mechanisms of control began to take new forms directed at the masses rather than individuals. The formation of the state and rationalization of the state is through a primary focus upon the population as a whole. While individualizing methods of control such as surveillance, obedience, and docility do not disappear from the state's range of possibility, techniques of power begin to center upon developing and controlling themes and patterns of the masses. In this way, the state simultaneously individualizes and totalizes its members (Foucault, 1981, p. 254).

Regulatory

Foucault establishes the birth of 'biopolitics' at the end of the eighteenth century as power and control shift from managing humans as individuals to populations. Emerging processes such as birth rate, mortality, longevity, and statistics characterize new ways of understanding populations. Biopolitics is the identification and intervention of phenomena and the construction of populations as political problems (Foucault, 1997, p. 243). The main concerns of biopolitics are matters of life and death, with birth and reproduction, health and sickness, both mental and physical, and with the actions that preserve or impede the optimization of a population. Thusly, biopolitics must involve "social, cultural, environmental, economic and geographic conditions under which humans live, procreate, become ill, maintain health or become healthy, and die" (Dean, 2010, p. 119). To maintain the security and well-being of the state, mechanisms of control that differ from disciplinary methods are introduced.

The functions of such mechanisms are very different from earlier disciplinary techniques. As Foucault (1997) explains, "The mechanisms introduced by biopolitics include forecasts, statistical estimates, and overall measures. And their purpose is...to intervene at the level at which these general phenomena are determined, to intervene at the level of their generality" (p. 246). This contrasts disciplinary mechanisms, which intend to modify a given phenomenon alone or a given individual independently. In this way, the state must intervene in such processes as stimulating the birth rate or increasing life expectancy. Involvement in biopolitical phenomena requires establishing regulatory mechanisms, which create equilibrium. There is security and safety in the development of control through societal stability.

In the milieu of biopolitics, it is no longer necessary to concern individuality as discipline does. To the contrary, using mechanisms and acting in ways that achieve regularity are of the utmost importance. "It is, in a word, a matter of taking control of life and the biological processes of man-as-species and of ensuring that they are not disciplined, but regularized" (Foucault, 1997, pp. 246–247). Similarly, Scheurich (1994) suggests "there is a grid of social regularities that constitutes what becomes socially visible as a social problem and what becomes socially visible as a range of credible...solutions" (p. 301). Social regularities exist as a powerful mechanism of control contributing to the inevitability of biopolitical processes. Public education as a governmental body is an ideal example of an institution that sets certain regularities as well as a range of possible solutions. For instance, a student is exhibiting behaviors deemed irregular and unfit for the classroom environment, specific practices and methods are implemented in response, and if no progress is made the child is moved to a different classroom or school that can better suit his needs. Standards of behavior are established by the governing body (school), interventions are set and measured by 'experts,' and protocol for environmental controls is followed. The course of action must progress in this manner, deviations are not acceptable, and suggestions that do not 'fit' the regularized pattern are not considered viable options.

Related to Scheurich's 'grids of social regularities' are Foucault's (1980) 'general politics of truth':

> Each society has its régime of truth, its 'general politics' of truth: that is, the types of discourse which it accepts and makes function as true; the mechanisms and instances which enable one to distinguish true and false statements, the means by which each is sanctioned; the techniques and procedures accorded value in the acquisition of truth; the status of those who are charged with saying what counts as true. (p. 131)

In terms of state control over the population, accepted discourse is a powerful method of authority. Governmentality encompasses the general politics of truth in society. Typically, these mechanisms are created by those in power (often through coercive measures to serve very narrow interests) and are disseminated to the public in subtle ways that ensure acceptance.

With the introduction of the technology of biopower, governmental bodies move from disciplinary methods of control like public displays of punishment to much more subtle measures. The key to successful governance is for populations themselves to become invested in their *own* discipline and regulation (Smythe, 2015, p. 225). This is the introduction of state control mechanisms such as 'technologies of the self' and the 'life-long learner.'

Forms of government develop indirect techniques of leading and controlling individuals. "The strategy of rendering individual subjects "responsible" entails shifting the responsibility for social risks such as illness, unemployment, poverty, etc. and for life in society into the domain for which the individual is responsible and transforming it into a problem of "self-care" (Lemke, 2002, p. 59). Such modification is a distant method of control from those associated with pastoral power and the welfare state. These technologies of the self are characteristic of an ever-increasing neoliberal government and are critical to the success of such a regime of power. Issues that were formerly treated as societal problems, such as poverty are now viewed as individual dilemmas. Social programs are eliminated and those who need public assistance are left to fend for themselves or remorsefully seek charity.

"A lifelong learner works actively in communities of learners and engages in a continuous course of personal responsibilities and self management of one's risks and destiny" (Fontaine & Luttrell, 2015, p. 51). Taking responsibility for one's own learning and self-management reinforces neoliberal ideology of individualization. Such practices are internalizations of governmental regulation and control. Bragg (2007) describes this notion as "an autonomous self that is capable of being worked on through various governmental 'technologies of the self'" (p. 345). Individuals have their independence and free will yet they remain compelled to adhere to and flourish within governmental constraints.

Values of being thoughtful and productive about uses of time as well as continuous self-improvement are deeply embedded in public institutions and structures such as schooling (Fontaine & Luttrell, 2015, p. 51). Students are taught at a very young age that success in school is measured by their willingness to not only conform to the system but to embrace personal responsibility for their learning. Self-regulation in terms of education removes the necessity for public schools (as extensions of the government) to provide equitable education; for students, and students alone, are responsible for their success or failure. A common sentiment among teachers is, "I taught it but he didn't learn it." This statement removes the teacher's obligation to teach and simultaneously places accountability upon the student for his own learning, reinforcing governmental control through technologies of the self.

"Governmentality implicates all of us, therefore, as active participants, who express our agency through both complicity and resistance to the circuits and regimes of power within which we live our lives" (Hamilton, Heydon, Hibbert, & Stooke, 2015, p. 4). The paradoxical notion that individuals can exist as both autonomous and influenced by mechanisms of control may allow space for contestation. I believe that such contested spaces exist in public institutions that are clearly affected by the reaches of governmentality.

Mitra, Mann, and Hlavacik (2016) define this concept of contested spaces as an educational context where ideas are shared and action is taken to challenge dominant social, political, or cultural ideologies that implicate learning and teaching in schools (p. 5). Such dominant ideologies are assuredly extensions of governmental notions as previously described. Foucault suggests people are freer than they think when they practice everyday resistance to everyday power (Martin, Gutman, & Hutton, 1988, pp. 10–11). These proposed ideas allow for hope and possibilities beyond the narrow regulatory regimes of power, which are often perceived as both perpetual and inevitable.

Resistance

Testing resistance is a theme that has and will continue to be suggested throughout this book. I would like to briefly provide a background for testing resistance as well as articulate some of the different ways students may resist testing. Neill (2016) proclaims that "Testing in the United States has been criticized since at least the first uses of IQ tests" (p. 16). In the 1970's serious opposition emerged to the use of IQ and SAT tests in the placement of Black youth into special education programs (Neill, 2016, p. 16).

In the late 1990's, Massachusetts began implementation of statewide exams in several grades as well as a graduation test, these exams set off significant resistance from parents and teachers. Along with a small number of schools in other states about the same time, the resistance in Massachusetts was the first large-scale opposition to standardized testing, including rather widespread opting-out. No Child Left Behind in 2002 with its negative consequences, testing errors, and cheating cases ignited opposition that slowly developed into today's resistance movement (Neill, 2016, p. 16).

In 2011, following the grassroots Save Our Schools March in Washington DC, United Opt Out began. This small group of activists radically advocated for not only opting-out of standardized testing but also "collective actions that would entirely dismantle corporate-driven education policy" (McDermott, 2015, pp. 22–23). As testing continued to become more invasive in public schools, opposition continued and encompassed the Common Core State Standards, loss of privacy as digital testing was mandated, and school closures (Neill, 2016, pp. 17–18). Resistance comes in many forms; from clear opt-out resistance to subtler conformist and silent resistance.

Envisioning the testing resistance movement, widespread opt-out, test refusal, and declining to administer standardized testing comes to mind. Those are all significant and arguably, quite influential ways in which students, parents, educators, and stakeholders can impact positive social change. On the other hand, actively not speaking about an issue is what Foucault might term 'counter-conduct.' "Foucault developed the term counter-conduct to designate forms of resistance to the practices and techniques of government forms of power" (Niesche, 2015, p. 140). When educators and students refuse to discuss things like negative school report cards, they are not bringing its effects into existence through spoken discourse and resisting the influence of the negative report card.

Similarly, San Pedro (2015) studied the ways that Native American students used their silence as a way to use agency to oppose assimilation and accommodation (p. 142). "Silence is used to shield students' identities from dominant paradigms that may be forced upon them at school" (San Pedro, 2015, p. 141).

In this way, not speaking about school issues that perpetuate marginalization is a form of resistance. Finally, Alpert (1991) found that students resisted through their conforming to school requirements (pp. 355–356). Students "going along" with school provisions, like participating in standardized testing, is a way to resist. They are complying with the school's modes of evaluation but remain concerned with their own rights and freedom of expression. Furthermore, these types of resistance must be revealed as they are extremely personal and unobservable in a general setting. This brief introduction to resistance is included to provide some foundational understanding of what resistance is and how I will be referring to it throughout this text.

In Research

Governmentality as a social theory can provide a wealth of understanding when applied to educational research. In this section, I will address some of the different ways scholars have utilized the theory of governmentality to enhance, explain, and interpret their research. In an effort to coherently organize this information, I will discuss the studies in a progressive fashion reflective of the first section: care through knowledge, individualization, regularizing, discourse and truth, and technologies of the self.

Care through Knowledge
Foucault's allegory of the shepherd is fundamental to understanding the governmental control mechanism of power as care through knowledge. This analogy can be applied in many different ways to diverse situations to help bring clarity to issues of power, control, and care with regard to knowledge. Within her discussion of vaccinations, Nadesan (2009) highlights the fact that parents are frequently harassed by health care providers who view alternative protocols as threatening both children and the nation's health. "Vaccinations have become a fundamental point of conflict between officials who *shepherd* the public's health and individuals who view their children as 'at risk' by widely practiced and mandated health technologies" (p. 388, emphasis added). I would like to call attention to Nadesan's reference to pastoral power. As Foucault (1981) established, the shepherd protects the salvation of his flock and the governmental body in this example is ensuring the health and welfare of the public through mandated vaccinations of the youth. Efforts to protect the wellbeing of individuals such as this are technologies of control.

Carlson's (2009) exploration of high-stakes portfolio assessment in Kentucky also speaks to power as care through knowledge. Using a governmentality lens,

Carlson (2009) determines that while the portfolio assessment is an alternative to the typical standardized test, it may not be as authentic as perceived. Although the portfolio appears to provide students greater opportunity to authentically express themselves freely as autonomous individuals, the effects of such assessments excise any humanistic intentions (p. 258).

> Making the student the owner, or sovereign of his/her work, and making the teacher the coach, or pastoral guide, represents a strategic way to produce neoliberal subjects who are independent, entrepreneurial subjects equipped to take care of themselves, and by doing so, allows the state to function. (Carlson, 2009, p. 263)

This is a very subtle usage of a governmental control mechanism. Care is disguised for the students by allowing them opportunities to develop their own portfolios. Then the portfolio entries are assessed against standards. The subsequent knowledge is used to sort and rank students based on their abilities. This is certainly an example of a covert strategy to express power as care through knowledge.

Individualization

Individualization is also a control mechanism characteristic of pastoral power. It is through a deep understanding of each member of his flock that the shepherd maintains his power over them. This notion can be applied to matters of education as Stickney (2009) has done in his study of teachers and the ways in which they navigate education reform efforts and regimes of inspection. He notes that pastoral supervision is manifested in teacher inspection systems. 'Supervision for growth' or 'annual growth' plans in which teachers confess their weaknesses to administrators and then establish benchmarks for their own professional development on the surface…can be self-empowering and transformative, or [more likely] self-indicating and servile" (Stickney, 2009, p. 250). Those in power gain intricate and personal understanding of each employee through such practices. According to The National Comprehensive Center for Teacher Quality (n.d.) ten states, including mine, specifically indicate usage of the Charlotte Danielson framework in teacher and principal evaluations. Within this evaluation system teachers are required to create individual growth plans, which focus upon a personal area of need and a plan of action to improve performance. Regimes of inspection such as these are governmental mechanisms of control.

Zipin and Brennan (2009) reference Foucault's view that the tendency of Western societies is to build a type of political sovereignty that would be "a government of all and of each, and whose concerns would be at once to 'totalize' and to 'individualize'" (p. 347). In the coming sections I will discuss these totalizing governmental controls: regularization and normalization through discourse and politics of truth and finally technologies of the self.

Normalization through Discourse

It would be impossible to explore Foucault's idea of normalization as a mechanism of control without speaking to the order of discourse as both a contributing factor and independent mechanism as well. Beasley (2009) studies governmentality through the discourse of youth. She traces the emergence of 'adolescence' as a terminology in the late 19th century along with its corresponding discursive development focusing on the abnormal and juvenile delinquency (p. 175). "Theories of adolescence…can be considered as the discursive effects of certain sets of social practices, of power/knowledge that occur across numerous contemporary social domains" (Beasley, 2009, p. 175). Perhaps most troubling about the establishment of such norms through adolescent development and psychological discourses was and continues to be their acceptance as inevitable truths in schools. The effect has been to label, diagnose, categorize, normalize, and judge children against these rules and specifications.

As Carlson (2009) explains, the development of neoliberal governments gave rise to the development of individuals in the state being governed 'through society' and through a 'social norm' (p. 259). They were able to sort out abnormal behavior and determine abnormalities as well as suggest solutions to correct them. "In short, experts begin to develop what Foucault calls, regimes of truth about whole populations and codify and disseminate information about normal experiences" (Carlson, 2009, p. 259). Educators are an example of such experts who assess, judge, categorize, and sort students through established norms and behaviors.

Graham (2009) articulates this idea in her analysis of ethnographic narratives of Australian children placed in alternative schools for intensive behavior modification programs. Using a governmentality lens, she examines vignettes as events where children are subjected to intense disciplinary action because their 'disorderly' behavior threatens to expose invisible relations of power and the falsity of 'choice.' Graham (2009) argues, "it is these norms and limits—structured by dominant social, cultural and political forces constituting the 'sovereignty of the good'—that ultimately take precedence" (p. 358). These forces can be understood as the discourse surrounding behavioral expectations of school. Graham determines that student needs are subordinate to the status quo.

Similarly, Nadesan (2009) speaks to the exclusion of autistic children from the regular classroom based on normalization. "The autistic child...has significant difficulty developing cultural disciplines and technologies of the self, characteristic of 'normal' children. Consequently, they are perceived as ungovernable. Their ungovernable may trigger disciplinary reprisals" (p. 390). In both cases (behavior and autism) children who function outside the socially established norms are subject to repercussions, which are commonly practiced through exclusion, alienation, and discipline.

Setting specific standards as measures with which to judge students is a common technology of control practiced within educational systems worldwide. Flewitt and Roberts-Holmes (2015) acknowledge the disciplinary effects of assessment technologies in their study of 'non-sense' phonics testing in early literacy in England (p. 95). The researchers conclude that the Phonics Screening Check is flawed as children are labeled either successful or failures. "It attempts to ensure that all young children conform to the same universal, comparable and certralised standards and at the same time it excludes complexity and diversity...normalizing certain children and categorizing others as being outside developmental norms" (Flewitt & Roberts-Holmes, 2015, p. 104). Assessments such as this, function as control mechanisms and are simultaneously established as 'best practice' procedures.

Albers, Harste, and Vasquez (2015) address normalization through standardization. Educators are frequently positioned to become docile bodies that implement scripted lessons with required standardized tests. These normalizing practices restrict creativity and innovation in the classroom. However, within contested spaces, educators can utilize alternative methods to teaching content (Albers et al., 2015, p. 115). And so, the authors recognize the prevalent normalization within schools yet offer resistance through critical and multimodal literacy curricula. Such a curriculum generates a

> space for educators to disrupt disciplinary techniques aimed to encourage docility and open up engagements that work against normalizing practices and expectations that serve national mandates and standards, standards that reflect the experiences of the few rather than the many. (Albers et al., 2015, p. 119)

These sentiments are common in the research; standards normalize through control, labeling, and sorting the population. The theory of governmentality helps studies such as this situate their findings and understand how these common and widely accepted practices operate in covert fashion.

Zipin and Brennan (2009) critically analyze the growing phenomenon of part-time secondary students in South Australia through a governmentality perspective. They stress that within Australia, as in other western nations, schools are viewed as producers of human capital to assure national growth and individual employment prospects from international organizations, state and national governments, businesses, and media outlets (Zipin & Brennan, 2009, p. 343). Pressures, standards, and norms are established and enacted through the discourse generated by the aforementioned entities. The rise in Southern Australian students choosing part-time schooling can be attributed to associated discourse's normalizing themes, that more qualifications and early work experiences are necessary for employment readiness in new knowledge economies (Zipin & Brennan, 2009, p. 343). This reality reflects control through both discursive action and pastoral power. Students presume they must obtain gainful job experience as well as a 'proper' education because the dominant discourse manifests such ideals. Concurrently, notions of pastoral power can be identified insofar as the governing body is constantly concerned with maintaining and advancing the good of the masses through individualization and ultimately technologies of the self. Chesky and Goldstein (2016) echo this notion, "Adolescents are to be studied, surveilled, and directly *acted upon* through particular interventions in order to shape their development as productive members of society" (p. 134). The utility of students as contributing citizens to the economic growth and well-being of the global marketplace is of great importance.

Technologies of the Self

Bragg's 2007 study explores the ways in which governmentality concepts assist in understanding how student voice initiatives play a central role in education policy. Not only do such practices perpetuate norms of individualism, they also support notions of self-reliance and self-management (p. 343). The authors investigate the initiative, *Students as Researchers* (SAR) as a way for students to investigate issues they determine as important to their educative experience (Bragg, 2007, p. 346). SAR encourages students to take responsibility for themselves and contribute to school success (Bragg, 2007, p. 352). "If SAR constitutes students as active, responsible, able to take charge of their own learning, then potentially, one also takes responsibility for one's failure to learn" (Bragg, 2007, p. 356). This conclusion is indicative of control through the neoliberal ideology of self-care.

Carlson's (2009) portfolio assessments reiterate the tendency to view students as solely accountable for their learning. Portfolio assessment

> encourages the students to make an investment in the self, one that demonstrates how one can engage in personal transformation…What is being measured in the writing portfolio is not just a student's writing abilities, but also their abilities to be independent owners of their work, and thus, entrepreneurs of oneself. (Carlson, 2009, p. 267)

The emphasis upon technologies of the self is critical to governmental power and control. Neoliberal ideology thrives upon the manifestation of technologies such as self-improvement and the life-long learner.

For Student Voice and Testing

Governmentality is a theoretical framework that informs my research. Testing continues to become more prevalent and pervasive in public schools and the principles of governmentality provide an ideal theoretical lens for this study. Consider Foucault's (1995) thoughts upon the examination,

> The examination combines the techniques of an observing hierarchy and those of a normalizing judgement. It is a normalizing gaze, a surveillance that makes it possible to qualify, to classify and to punish. It establishes over individuals a visibility through which one differentiates them and judges them. That is why, in all the mechanisms of discipline, the examination is highly ritualized. In it are combined the ceremony of power and the establishment of truth…We are entering the age of the infinite examination and of compulsory objectification. (pp. 184, 189)

The current emphasis upon quality, control, and accountability within education systems around the world reflects Foucault's thoughts on the examination. The era in which universal standards are implemented and assessed to control the population is our current reality. Hibbert (2015) considers this notion in her exploration of freedom in the context of Shakespearean curriculum of Canadian secondary students (pp. 149–152). She contends, the most significant factor driving the 'governed' mentality was the implementation of standardized assessments and reporting systems. Media presented the results and ranked schools based on student performance. "Boards of Education across the province responded with a focus on 'data' and results in ways that obscured meaningful dialogue about authentic, situated teaching and learning" (p. 153). These practices are comparable to the American reality of Common Core State

Standards and aligned assessments such as the PARCC test. In any case, power through control, normalizing, and individual knowledge is pervasive in such practices.

Albers et al. (2015) explain that the Common Core State Standards encourage argumentation and written language over imagination and creativity. Further, it can be assumed that 'common' refers to the mythical American 'norm' of white, middle-class values. "Within a Foucauldian perspective, normalization is a key technique of disciplinary power and non-conformity results in punishment" (Albers et al., 2015, p. 125). There are incidents across the country of teachers and students who endure negative consequences as a direct effect of the normalizing practice of standardization such as job loss, retention, expulsion, and various sanctions.

"Power deployed as governmentality is pervasive in institutions, such as schools" (Taylor & Robinson, 2009, p. 171). It becomes less about the actual or physical government enforcing mandates like high-stakes testing and more about how and why it is necessary for *you* (the student, the teacher, the principal, the parent, the community, the state) to do well on those exams. Smith (2014) expands the influence of governmentality beyond the individual in his discussion of the global transformation toward testing for accountability.

> Testing for accountability is so engrained in many countries that it is partially self-perpetuating. The use of assessment data reinforces the testing culture and the public view of testing for accountability as synonymous with high expectations makes it challenging for policymakers to alter established practices, whether or not they want to, in fear of constituents labelling them soft on education. (p. 20)

Governmental control embodied in the power structures of education systems can be challenging to discern as it is rooted in the nature of public school itself. However, for the purposes of this argument, the influence of Foucault's governmentality is evident in the perpetual acceptance and use of high-stakes standardized exams.

Additionally, Lemke (2002) considers Foucault's discussion of neoliberal governmentality as an extension of government; neoliberalism is a transformation of politics that changes the power relationships in society.

> What we observe today is not a diminishment or a reduction of state sovereignty and planning capacities but a displacement from formal to informal techniques of government and the appearance of new actors

on the scene of government, that indicate fundamental transformations in statehood and a new relation between state and civil society anchors. (Lemke, 2002)

It is through this neoliberal lens that testing conglomerates like Pearson Inc. (creator of the PARCC test) wield power and control over schools across the globe. Schneider (2015) explains, "[Pearson] offers services, as well as content, from test creation, administration and processing to teacher development and school software. It operates in more than 70 countries worldwide its major markets are the United States (55% of sales) and Europe (22% of sales)" (pp. 177–178). This form of power can be described as an informal technique of government. The federal legislation of No Child Left Behind (NCLB) stipulation that any state receiving Title I funds must adhere to high-stakes exams through federally approved consortia: PARCC or Smarter Balanced Assessment Consortia (SBAC). Schools in all fifty states as well as Puerto Rico and the District of Columbia receive Title I monies.

Crowder and Konle (2015) discuss the notion that Pearson has "situated itself as part of the state enforcement apparatus presumably performing their duties in accordance with the will of the people" (p. 286). In 2015, a superintendent in New Jersey was contacted by officials at the New Jersey Department of Education concerning a testing security breach during a PARCC exam. As it turned out, after school hours a student tweeted content that referenced a PARCC test question. The Department of Education noted that Pearson was monitoring all social media for references to the PARCC test. The publishing company's statement about this matter reads, "Pearson is contractually required by states to monitor public conversations on social media to ensure that no assessment information (text, photos, etc.) that is secure and not public is improperly disclosed" (Crowder & Konle, 2015, pp. 285–286). And so, Pearson can spy on students' social media postings as they are a self-proclaimed extension of the government.

Consider Foucault's (1991) explanation of govermentalization,

> The governmentalization of the state is at the same time what has permitted the state to survive, and it is possible to suppose that if the state is what it is today, this is so precisely thanks to this governmentality, which is at once internal and external to the state, since it is the tactics of government which make possible the continual definition and redefinition of what is within the competence of the state and what is not, the public versus private and so on; thus the state can only be understood in its

survival and its limits on the basis of the general tactics of governmentality. (p. 103)

By Foucault's own admission the state itself is legitimized through acts of government. Allow me to put this in terms that are relatable to the present discussion. The federal government in effect has no power until laws constitute it. For example, the State Board of Education is merely an inconsequential entity until it can enforce actions of the state, such as mandating PARCC testing in public schools. As Foucault specifies, *it is the tactics of government which make possible the continual definition and redefinition of what is within the competence of the state and what is not*. These "tactics of government" may come in the form of formal legislation such as Every Student Succeeds Act (ESSA) or independent school policy or they may be subtler as the inevitability of accountability in schools. Nevertheless, the influence of governmentality as a theoretical principle for the present work, provides a necessary foundation upon which to build the prevalence high-stakes testing in the US.

As I have reviewed the literature I have found two ways in which governmentality plays a role in the concept of student voice (1) students are conditioned in ways that may influence their capacity to change and (2) student expressions can be utilized in ways that favor the dominant ideology of a school or practice. First, McIntyre et al. (2005) found that "Committed teachers need to remember that pupils will need adequate opportunities to learn how to undertake new responsibilities" (p. 167). Through their experimental research, they found that on occasion when students were given a great proportion of planning and managing responsibilities they were not adequately prepared and both behavior and academic issues developed. It is only through experience that students are able to function with such obligations, typically children have been 'schooled' to listen to the teacher and follow his/her directions without room for variation. In this way, the influence of governmentality as classroom expectancy is evident. Additionally, Bragg (2007) discusses the notion that "Student voice now appears to be…intentionally or not masking the "real" interests of those in power…using pupil voice as an additional mechanism of control" (p. 344). This is materialized in student surveys of curriculum or practice that manipulate choices or results to support or oppose an educational practice. Consider the following survey questions students are asked at the conclusion of the PARCC test,

13. Was it easy to use the highlighter?
    Yes, it was easy
    No, it was hard I did not use the highlighter

14. Was it easy to make pictures or words bigger or smaller?
    Yes, it was easy
    No, it was hard I did not change the size of pictures or words

15. Was it easy to move back and forth between passages or stories?
    Yes, it was easy
    No, it was hard I did not move between passages or stories

One issue is the limited response choices. With the omission of any degree choice, students feel that they have to answer yes or no, when perhaps it was easy at one point during the test and difficult at another. Additionally, these questions are worded with a positive connotation; "was it easy" is repeated (and these were not the only questions worded in this manner). They are designed to sway the respondent in the affirmative, "It was easy, wasn't it?" Keep in mind, the students participating in this 23-question survey have just taken 75–90 minute English Language Arts high-stakes exam on some sort of electronic device and they are anywhere between 8 and 18 years old. Armed with student voice input from surveys like these, the makers and proponents of the PARCC test can manipulate the data to support their cause.

The theory of governmentality adds depth to understanding the ways in which standardization and assessment practices play a great role in public education. Certainly, the various aspects of Foucault's theory of governmentality (biopolitics, normalization, and self-care to name a few) have clear correlation to testing in public schools. The reaches of governmentality can be applied to every aspect of standardized testing and student experience, which is why I have chosen to ground my research with this social theory. As you will later read, I build upon these tenets in the analysis of my research to create a clear understanding of the ways students are manipulated and controlled through standardized assessment practices in public schools.

CHAPTER 5

The Study

> *The point of critical research is generally to do research* with *people, not* on *people.*
> MERRIAM AND TISDELL (2016, p. 64)

∴

Methods

The following research was designed as a critical qualitative case study. This type of investigation explores human phenomena that cannot be sufficiently explored through quantitative methods. Carspecken (1996) elaborates, "Critical" qualitative research is one of several genres of inquiry into nonquantifiable features of social life" (p. 3). Additionally, critical researchers share values concerning social inequities and social theories involving social structure, culture, power, and human agency (Carspecken, 1996, p. 3). My work purposefully engaged students in dialogue to promote human agency through student voice. Further, I view these conversations regarding standardized assessment between students and myself as a phenomenon that cannot and should not be quantified.

Characterizing the critical nature of critical social research is complex. In their summary of the work of critical researchers Kinchloe and McLaren (1994) note many distinguishing points, among them,

> We are defining a criticalist as a researcher or theorist who attempts to use her or his work as a form of social or cultural criticism and who accepts certain basic assumptions...that certain groups in any society are privileged over others and, although the reasons for this privileging may vary widely, the oppression which characterizes contemporary societies is most forcefully reproduced when subordinates accept their social status as natural, necessary, or inevitable. (as cited in Carspecken, 1996, p. 4)

This notion directly speaks to my critical research because (1) standardized assessment measures historically oppress marginalized groups, which

© KONINKLIJKE BRILL NV, LEIDEN, 2019 | DOI: 10.1163/9789004401365_005

duplicate the status quo and (2) acceptance of phenomena as natural or inevitable is a fundamental principle of Foucault's theory of governmentality.

Critical researchers not only share values but also have a common concern over epistemological issues as well. "Critical epistemology does not give us a recipe for helping the poor and downtrodden; it rather gives us principles for conducting valid inquiries into any area of human experience" (Carspecken, 1996, p. 8). Critical epistemology operates with the notion that some are benefiting while others are marginalized. There is a critique to be made regarding the ways we come to know things. My research stems from a critical epistemological foundation insofar as it challenges the status quo; current standardized assessment practices in public schools.

As previously alluded to, my experience with standardized assessments left me with many questions. I gained valuable insight to these questions through the student interviews and data analysis. Carspecken (1996) indicates that criticalists have reconsidered traditional ideas about knowledge and reality, finding them lacking (p. 6). I believe I am this person. I have reevaluated what I thought and believed about assessment practices in public schools and found them deficient in numerous ways. The critical perspective of critical qualitative research with its concerns of power and human agency make it an ideal approach to my study.

Case Study Research

The methodology for this research is critical case study. Yin (2003) explains, "As a research strategy, the case study is used in many situations to contribute to our knowledge of individual, group, organizational, social, political and related phenomena" (p. 1). It is my hope that this study contributes to our knowledge of individual (students), group (grade levels, schools), organizational (district), social (public schooling), and political (mass standardized testing production) phenomena.

While there are many research strategies in the social sciences, I have chosen critical case study based partially upon Yin's (2003) *Relevant Situations for Different Research Strategies* table (p. 5). In this figure (and following description) Yin (2003) compares experiment, survey, archival analysis, history, and case study strategies in three categories: Form of Research Question, Requires Control of Behavioral Events?, and Focuses on Contemporary Events?. According to Yin (2003) case study asks 'how, why' questions, does not require control of behavioral events, and focuses on contemporary events. My research questions, extent of investigator control, and degree of focus on contemporary as opposed to historical events certainly reflect Yin's criteria for case study research.

The inquiry method of critical case study was purposefully utilized in this qualitative study in an effort to gain an understanding of the ways students view testing practices in public schools including purpose, function, and resistance. Case study is defined as an empirical inquiry that
- investigates a contemporary phenomenon within its real-life context, especially when
- the boundaries between phenomenon and context are not clearly evident (Yin, 2003, p. 13).

Standardized testing, as a phenomenon cannot be removed from its real-life context, the school. This is evidenced through the lens of governmentality as applied to this study. The questions I am asking in this work cannot be removed from their context to focus on specific variables.

Case study is a practical approach to this research, as case study inquiry "copes with the technically distinctive situation in which there will be many more variables of interest than data points, and as one result relies on multiple sources of evidence" (Yin, 2003, pp. 13–14). Yin (2003) cites six sources of evidence: documentation, archival records, interviews, direct observations, participant-observation, and physical artifact (p. 86). In this study, the primary source of data was collected through individual semi-structured interviews with students. Additionally, I directly observed the three classrooms of the six participants a total of nine times (three observations in each grade 3, 5, and 8) for approximately 40 minutes each observation session. Finally, as an employee of the district from which the research was conducted, I was able to obtain physical artifacts as documents regarding testing practices, procedures, and schedules. Ultimately, I drew from these multiple sources of evidence to theorize about the process of students becoming obedient, controlled, and manipulated through a governmentality perspective as reflected in their compliance with testing.

Researcher Positionality

As a social science researcher, it is important for me to reflect upon my personal position, bias, and conflict of interest with regard to my subjects and the topics of this study. Carspecken (1996) explains, statements of "fact," in research, are affected by values and thusly can never be strictly "neutral" or "objective." Therefore, critical epistemology must make the fact—value distinction clear and also have a precise understanding of how the two interact. This understanding allows researchers to develop standards by which to avoid or reduce bias in their work (p. 9). While I have not claimed to have found "facts" in my analysis, I do theorize and I like to believe, that by understanding the ways in which my values may have affected this research I have reduced bias in my findings.

As an established teacher of twelve years in the school district where this research took place, I have a conflict of interest. While I have never taught the students who participated in my study, they likely know who I am. And as an educator in the district, I am interested in the learning of all our students. As stated in the Parent Guardian Letter of Consent, I clearly identified my conflict of interest, "The person responsible for this research study is a teacher in ____ District at ____ School and is interested in your child's learning as an educator at the school as well as the conduct of this study." While I do not think it will affect the study, I wanted to openly articulate this notion.

Next, through my experience with standardized assessment as both a participant and administrator, I have come to adopt a negative view of them. My graduate work and ensuing research have contributed to this unfavorable perspective of public school standardized testing. However, I was very conscientious of this fact when I interviewed the participants in my study and in formulating my interview questions. I was meticulous in developing questions that would not covertly express my bias. For example, the first lead off question I asked students was, "Tell me about taking the PARCC test. Walk me through what is was like using as much detail as possible." And a possible follow-up question like, "So, you had to take the test on the computer. Tell me more about that." With questions like these I intended to have participants discuss a concrete example, which would lend itself to the abstract domains I was hoping to learn about with as little of my personal bias present as possible.

As previously referred to, Paulo Freire's theory of critical pedagogy greatly influenced the design of this study. Specifically, I aimed to engage participants in purposeful dialogue that would give them power over their current situation. Through my introduction of this study to the participating classes, the Parent/Guardian Letter of Consent, Student Letter of Assent, and the interview process itself, I conveyed the importance of the empowerment of student voice as a guiding principle and significant personal value.

Upon my first visit to each of the three classrooms from where I drew participants, I explained who I was, what I was doing, and why it was important to me to conduct interviews with kids. In the consent and assent letters, I expressed my position on student voice through statements like, "I believe students have an underrepresented yet important role in educational research," "I am interested in your child's thoughts and opinions," and "I believe that kids your age have a lot of interesting things to say." I was mindful of the possibility that students might not be comfortable talking one-on-one with me as I was not (and never was) their teacher, I am an adult, they have likely never participated in an interview or research study, etc. Consequently, I made every effort to make the interview process as enjoyable and relaxed as possible. Before and after asking questions from the Interview Protocol I tried to get to know the students by engaging them in conversations about themselves and telling them about myself. Additionally, I offered the students snacks and water as these interviews took place right after school and they were likely hungry. I wanted the kids to feel at ease, I tried to use uncomplicated language, smile, laugh, and clarify for understanding. I hope that I was able to convey my position on student voice throughout the research process.

Means

The Participants

In this study, I sought to engage students in conversations about their experiences with standardized testing. One of the elements I was interested in was how their responses may change over time, which is why I enrolled participants in varied grades. State-mandated testing begins in grade 3 and I work in a district that serves students kindergarten through eighth grade. I decided to try and find student participants from grades 3, 5, and 8 to give stratified points of view from this population of opportunity.

One of the first criteria established was that I would not interview students from my current class of third graders to avoid any type of concern or coercion. The selection process was random and was based on the first two students from each grade level to return the signed consent forms, therefore I could not control whether or not participants from grades five and eight were my former students. As it turned out, I had never taught any of the students who participated in my research. Once the selection process was planned, I approached teachers I thought would be open to participating and with whom I had worked with closely in the past. Mrs. Frost is a third grade teacher and we worked on the same grade level team for eight years. Mrs. Jones is a fifth grade teacher with whom I co-taught my first two years of teaching. And Mrs. Mackley (the eighth grade teacher) served on one of the same committees as I had for a couple of years. Gratefully, these teachers were very open to my research, ensuing classroom observations, and the participant selection process.

I began the classroom observation process immediately and over approximately three weeks I was able to observe each classroom on three separate occasions for about 40 minutes each session. Upon my first visit to each classroom, the teachers allowed me a few minutes to introduce my study and myself. I explained the study's purpose, my reasoning behind interviewing kids, and the selection process. All students in each classroom were given a packet including both the Parent Consent and Student Assent forms. I was explicit in explaining that whether or not they decided to be in my study there would be no consequences whatsoever.

Thankfully, within a couple of weeks two participants from each grade level agreed to the interviews and returned all of the properly signed forms. As the students returned the forms, I scheduled the interviews with the students' parents because they were taking place after school hours and transportation would have to be provided by the family. Surprisingly, at a schoolwide book fair, a parent who has children in our district approached me about her eighth grade daughter participating in my study. She had heard from another teacher in our district what I was working on and thought that hearing what kids had to say about the PARCC test was a good idea. I agreed to interview her daughter, which is why I have three eighth grade participants.

The first two third grade students to return their forms were both female. I have assigned the White third grade student the pseudonym of "Emily" and the Hispanic third grade student the pseudonym of "Lexie." The two fifth grade participants who returned forms were both White males. I have assigned the fifth grader interviewed first the pseudonym of "Chris" and the fifth grader interviewed third the pseudonym "Gary." The first eighth grade participant to return the forms was a White male whom I have given the pseudonym of "Sal." The second eighth grade participant to return the forms was an Arab female whom I have given the pseudonym of "Ana." And finally, the unexpected eighth grade participant was a White female whom I have given the pseudonym of "Brooke." Brooke was a student at the junior high in our district but was not in Mrs. Mackley's homeroom class from which I drew the participants.

Generation of Data

This research utilized both classroom observations and semi-structured interviews for the data collection process. The classroom observations took place over approximately three weeks and I visited each classroom for about forty minutes on three separate occasions. During each classroom's initial observation, I detailed who I was, why I was conducting my research, the participant selection process, and interview procedures (i.e. afterschool hours, approximately 45 minutes long, etc.). These observations generated a primary record in my recording journal. I developed the thick description by first drawing a picture of the setting including student-seating arrangements. The teachers provided me a class-seating chart, which I coded with numbers for each student. This way I was able to identify students easily without revealing (or having to write) their names, as I did not know who the participants would be, I carefully observed the entire class and detailed as much as I possibly could in the time I had. Carspecken (1996) explains that a thick description includes both context notes and a thick record (p. 46). For each observation, I detailed exact times, descriptions of the physical setting and student arrangements, as well as any other relevant information before I began generating the thick record.

Despite beginning classroom observations prior to participant selection, I still utilized Carspecken's Method of Priority Observation occasionally in my thick record. Carspecken (1996) explains that when employing the priority observation method, the researcher chooses one person in the setting to record everything that person does and says as thickly as possible as a first priority. Then records everything other people say and do in interaction with this person as a second priority and records everything else happening in the setting as a third priority (pp. 48–49). I observed these three classrooms as much as I possibly could; my time was limited to my plan periods and lunch breaks as I had a class of students myself. Further, it was after the administration of the PARCC test, which was the end of April and very close to the end of the school year, especially for eighth grade students as they graduated even earlier than the district end date of June first.

Beyond these nine observations, perhaps the more significant generation of data came from the seven one-on-one semi-structured student interviews. Once a student returned his/her consent and assent forms properly completed, I contacted the parent via phone or email (parents indicated their preferred method of contact on the consent form). I was extremely flexible in scheduling but most students were able to meet promptly. The interviews took place in my classroom after school was dismissed. An eighth interview fell outside these parameters. The fifth grade students participated in a pilot test for the Next Generation Science Standards of which our state has newly adopted. Following administration, I contacted Mrs. Jones, the fifth grade teacher, to schedule a time I could interview both fifth grade participants in an interactive group session regarding this standardized assessment. While I did not create an interview protocol to guide the discussion I engaged the boys in a conversation about the most recent test they had taken and used this data in my final analysis. All interviews were audio recorded. Students from the building in which I worked simply walked to my classroom after dismissal. I arranged to meet eighth grade students outside my school building on the playground that separates the elementary building from the junior high. When interviews concluded at approximately 3:45pm parents either picked up their children at the front office or the students had permission to walk home. There were no incidents with students getting to the interview or getting home afterward.

The data collection process emphasized the dissertation study's questions:
– How do students view their time spent on preparation for testing and participation in testing?

- How do students understand the purpose of testing; What is/are the function(s) of testing; Are there personal, school-wide, district-wide, state-wide, etc. benefits or consequences and how do students perceive the impact or lack thereof?
- If students questioned or resisted testing and in what ways?
- Did student responses change over time (across grades three, five, and eight)?

Overt and covert categories served to uncover students' knowledge and understanding of standardized assessment practices in public schooling. Overt categories consisted of attitudes and feelings regarding standardized testing as well as understandings of the policies mandating such testing practices. Covert categories included the ways in which students have become obedient, controlled, and manipulated through their compliance with standardized testing, resistance, and the ways responses may differ across grade levels.

The interview protocol I developed and utilized for each interviewee included two topic domains with two lead-off questions. Each lead-off question had three possible follow-up questions attached. While I generally adhered to this protocol I would ask students probing questions accordingly. For example, if students began talking about the district-wide standardized assessment, the NWEA MAP test (Northwest Evaluation Association Measures of Academic Progress), I would not cut them off.

Analysis and Interpretation

The final step within the methods process is analysis and interpretation. In preparation for the analysis and interpretation of data generated from the classroom observations and the digitally recorded individual interviews, I transcribed the interview recordings. This extremely time-consuming process was completed over several weeks. Finally, I was ready to begin my analysis and interpretation of the data generated using Carspecken's (1996) critical qualitative research methods and stages for data analysis and interpretation. This model helps researchers who strive to identify and analyze power relations (Carspecken, 1996, p. 40). Issues of power are directly related to my theoretical framework and design.

Carspecken (1996) notes that his five-stage scheme is meant to be generally appropriate for most qualitative research designs and portions of these five stages can be used separately (p. 40). I chose to make use of Stage One: compiling the primary record and Stage Three: reconstructive analysis, as they aligned with my purposes (Carspecken, 1996, pp. 41–42).

In the first stage, I built a primary record of the data consisting of a thick record and field journal notes, which were less detailed. My primary record included both field journal notes taken during and after the interviews as well as a thick record of classroom observations and transcribed student interviews. Once I established a primary record of the data, I began analysis using Carspecken's (1996) methods. I utilized a diverse set of techniques to "determine interaction patterns, their meanings, power relations, roles, interactive sequences, evidence of embodied, [and] intersubjective structures" (p. 42). There are three main steps within this second stage of analysis: (1) Coding, (2) Meaning Reconstruction, and (3) Pragmatic Horizon Analysis (Carspecken, 1996, pp. 146–153; pp. 94–102; pp. 103–125). I completed these steps in a mostly sequential order as they, to some extent, build off of one another.

This coding process helped me clarify the focus of my analysis. Carspecken (1996) suggests that once a thick set of codes is created, researchers can begin reorganization by grouping certain codes into a few large categories (p. 151). As an elemental focus of this study, Foucault's theory of governmentality undoubtedly influenced the ways in which I grouped these codes. Occasionally codes fell into more than one category and I found it necessary to create intermediate categories as well.

I began initial meaning construction through my transcription of the student interviews. As Carspecken (1996) suggests, "you ought to begin meaning construction by reading through the primary record and mentally noting possible underlying meanings" (p. 95). As I worked through the coding process, I selected several segments for specific, initial meaning reconstruction. I chose these selections because they were representative of action patterns. Additionally, I selected a few anomalies in the patterns as I thought they may be revealing of the underlying norms of more routine events (Carspecken, 1996, p. 95). I worked to reconstruct implicit meaning to make it explicit for the actors in the study through the development of meaning fields.

The last step in Carspecken's reconstructive data analysis I worked through was Pragmatic Horizon Analysis. Through this process I attempted to articulate implicit truth claims by differentiating between objective, subjective, and normative truth claims in the data.

Summary

My work has been designed as a critical qualitative research study. The critical perspective of critical qualitative research with its concerns of power and human agency make it an ideal approach to my study. The methodology for this research is critical case study. As a social science researcher, it is important for me to reflect upon my personal position, bias, and conflict of interest with regard to my subjects and the topics of this study. Seven participants from grades three, five, and eight were randomly selected for individual audio-recorded interviews. This study utilized both classroom observations and semi-structured interviews for the data collection process. For the analysis and interpretation of the data generated I used Carspecken's (1996) critical qualitative research methods and stages for data analysis and interpretation.

CHAPTER 6

What the Kids Have to Say

> *Through their first-hand knowledge and perspectives, students have the capacity to reveal ways we can effectively enact change in schools. We must listen to them to leverage educational reform.*
> DIERA (2016, p. 231)

∴

A primary purpose of my research was to raise awareness of student experiences and perspectives of standardized testing. Additionally, beyond an understanding of student perspectives this study served to interrogate if students were manipulated, regulated, and/or disciplined to view standardized testing as a natural part of what it means to be a public school student and if so, how these mechanisms of control presented themselves.

Furthermore, I considered how student views regarding standardization may change as they are promoted through the grades. Specifically, the ways in which students have or have not internalized control through assessment over time is explored. Ultimately, the purpose of this study was to theorize about the process of students becoming obedient, controlled, and manipulated through a governmentality lens as reflected in their compliance with testing.

I have organized this chapter by first, reporting the findings of my research beginning with classroom observations followed by individual student's big ideas. The next portion discusses common overarching themes that developed through my analysis. Six common themes of standardized assessment practice in public schools that emerged in this research include: (1) adverse attitudes, feelings, and experiences with testing practices, (2) purposes and consequences of standardized assessments, (3) the ways that standardized tests are used to normalize through labeling and sorting student populations, (4) the ways in which students exhibit obedience, (5) student references to a hierarchy of power and control in schools, and (6) technologies of the self. After which, I discuss the theme of resistance, which was specific to the eighth grade participants.

These common themes provide us with insights into testing practices in public schools today and how students are governed, manipulated, and controlled through the standardization process. The common themes I developed are informed by governmentality and student voice literature and build upon the literature through the experiences of seven public school children. Finally, I will discuss four ways that student responses change over time, across grades three, five, and eight.

By Grade Level

Third Grade

In our school building, there are three classrooms at each grade level. I have taught third grade with Mrs. Frost for eight years. My relationship with her and my understanding of her as an educator led me to feel comfortable asking her and her class to assist me in my research. Mrs. Frost was very receptive to my requests and I began classroom observations promptly.

Mrs. Frost has been teaching for 25 years in third grade for most of her career with the exception of five years in second grade. She has always taught all academic subjects (Reading, Math, English Language Arts, Science, and Social Studies) in the general education classroom. Mrs. Frost taught our Gifted and Academically Talented (GAT) students in third grade for 10 years, they were included in her general education classroom. She received her Master's degree in 2006 in Technology in the Classroom from a Midwestern university. Additionally, Mrs. Frost was the director for the GAT Program for 4 years until its dissolution.

My three classroom observations took place in the afternoons when Mrs. Frost was teaching Math and each lasted approximately 40 minutes. I formulated a thick record of observation and periodically utilized Carspecken's (1996) Method of Priority Observation (pp. 48–49). As these interviews took place prior to knowing whom my participants would be I took meticulous notes on all members of the class.

I found a small table in the back of the room from which I could survey the entire room and tried to make my presence as unobtrusive as possible. During my first visit, Mrs. Frost was reviewing a lesson on triangles from the day before. One of the first notable occurrences was that four students (who obviously did well on the lesson and did not need the extra instruction) were removed from the classroom to play a math game. This, in and of itself, is not unusual as teachers often differentiate instruction based on student ability, what piqued my interest was the ways that Mrs. Frost addressed and interacted with the students who remained in the classroom for additional support.

To begin, Mrs. Frost gently told students in the classroom, "the rest of us need a little help" as she handed back the students' previously completed work (personal communication, April 26, 2016). This was arguably the kindest way Mrs. Frost addressed the students during my entire first observation. Next, the English Language Learner (ELL) teacher came to take the students she services for instruction and Mrs. Frost refused to let them go, "We're redoing a paper we bombed out on" (personal communication, April 26, 2016). This comment was audible to me in the back of the classroom and assumedly to all of the students who "bombed" their assignment.

Students were extremely quiet during my visit, which I took extra notice of, as my class across the hall was completely different. Mrs. Frost began showing the students how to measure the sides of triangles and asked the students if they saw and understood what she was teaching them. The students stared in her direction and some nodded, to which Mrs. Frost responded that she could not understand why they turned in what they did. "You're not going to get out of doing the assignment by rushing" (Mrs. Frost, personal communication, April 26, 2016). The lesson continued, Mrs. Frost went through the questions and students compliantly worked at erasing and redoing their workbook page from the day before.

Mrs. Frost had two female students whom she 'calls out' quite often for various offenses like inattention, shouting out, not listening, not following directions, etc. but they are not the only ones. During this first observation, one of the girls was called upon for an answer despite not having her hand up to do so. She reluctantly cleared her throat and responded incorrectly to which Mrs. Frost responded, "This is how you were listening the first time we did this, that's why we're doing it again" (personal communication, April 26, 2016). The students seemed to be accustomed to this type of communication with their teacher as they calmly accepted her comments with little to no affect.

It was very clear to me that Mrs. Frost was upset with her class during this re-teach lesson. The subjective-referenced truth claim I am making here, is that Mrs. Frost seemed to believe that the students' lack of understanding and performing was their personal fault as evidenced by her interaction, tone, and delivery throughout my observation. While the students appeared to be listening and acting as though they were paying attention, I wondered if they were or if this was merely expected classroom behavior to avoid reprimand from their teacher.

I went into my next third grade observation a week later hopeful that Mrs. Frost's disposition in the previous lesson was due to the fact that she had to take the time to re-teach material and that this lesson would go better for the students. I was wrong. Mrs. Frost was reviewing attributes of quadrilaterals on a workbook page she and the class were working through together. Students were immediately scolded for incorrect responses among various other things.

One of Mrs. Frost's chosen two answered a question wrong, "Oh gosh, I wish you were listening" (Mrs. Frost, personal communication, May 2, 2016). Soon after, the teacher called on another female student who did not volunteer. Mrs. Frost asked the student to point to where they were right now (on the paper), she didn't know and was scolded for having written the last answer done together in the wrong spot on the page. "I'm sorry you can't follow along—that's too bad for you" (Mrs. Frost, personal communication, May 2, 2016).

Again, during this lesson, the students appeared to be paying attention but as Mrs. Frost points out, they are not,

> Boys and girls this is what's happening now—we're waiting for someone else to give us the answer—we're not even paying attention. I don't think I'm going to help the kids who haven't been paying attention. We'll see if those who haven't been listening can do 4 or 5. (personal communication, May 2, 2016)

In my observer comments, I noted that this sentiment was obvious, the kids were not engaged; they were silent and working on their papers but appeared to be "spaced out."

There are several hypotheses to address the students' lack of performance on this or even the previously observed lesson. Perhaps it is the direct instruction method of teaching, student engagement, time of day, content, etc. But one thing was very clear; again Mrs. Frost believed her students were to blame for their deficiency. For example, as students completed the front side of their workbook page they were to turn it over. Mrs. Frost approached a girl who was done and flipped here paper to check it. The student was promptly berated for having the wrong answer, "A square? This is a square? You're just writing down any nonsense." "No," the student softly responds. "Clearly you are" (Mrs. Frost, personal communication, May 2, 2016). And Mrs. Frost walked away without helping or guiding the student to the answer she was looking for.

My final observation took place two weeks later and again the class was going over the answers to a chapter review of polygons. The teacher called on a student who read the question and offered his/her answer. The teacher gave a brief explanation and called on the next student with his/her hand up to do the following question. As I noted in my observer comments, going through this work was very boring and I saw very little benefit to the amount of class time taken. Again, the class was silent during the entire exchange, mostly looking in the teacher's direction or at their papers. There were very little distractions occurring presumably because when they did take place Mrs. Frost would immediately reprimand or threaten the student. Like, "If you don't stop playing around I'm taking Field Day—feet on the ground—turn around" (Mrs. Frost, personal communication, May 16, 2016). These observations took place at the end of the school year and it was obvious that the teacher had set certain expectations for classroom behavior and deviations were unacceptable.

These classroom observations were very surprising to me. I was taken aback by Mrs. Frost's harsh tone and the exceptionally obedient climate of her classroom. Students never strayed from the class procedures and/or expectations. They were very submissive in their roles as receivers of information from their teacher. Not once did I witness a student exhibit any questioning, pushback, or resistance as traditionally conceived to the classroom content, practices, or procedures. However, the students were clearly "going through the motions," which may have been evidence of conformist resistance.

The students in Mrs. Frost's class appeared to be docile and compliant. This can be evidenced by their respect as perpetually silent, well-trained to the classroom rules and expectations, and lack of independence. Upon my analysis of these field notes, I repeatedly recorded the words 'obedient' and 'obedience,' which I have come to recognize as the overarching theme for these third grade classroom observations. Obedience is a disciplinary control mechanism and is clearly used as such by Mrs. Frost with her third graders.

Fifth Grade

Students in fifth grade switch classrooms for academic instruction in Science, Social Studies, and English Language Arts. Additionally, students may go to a different classroom for Mathematics instruction based on their achievement. I approached Mrs. Jones, a fifth grade teacher to participate in my study. This choice was made based on our relationship as co-teachers from 2005–2007. She was happy to help me with my participant selection and classroom observations. Mrs. Jones has been teaching for 27 years. All except 3 months she has been in 5th grade. Mrs. Jones began her career as a "Chapter 1" teacher in another district for the beginning of a school year. There she taught reading, math, and writing to low achieving students in K-8. She was then hired here, in our school, for a maternity leave in November of 1990. Mrs. Jones taught science to at least two classes every year and then reading, spelling, English, math, and writing to her homeroom. For a couple of years, she taught social studies as well.

Unfortunately, the times for my observations could not work as I was limited to my lunch and afternoon plan periods and her homeroom switched to Social Studies class with Mrs. Brooks. Mrs. Brooks has taught fifth grade for fifteen years at our school in all academic subject areas. Thankfully, Mrs. Brooks was willing to allow me to observe Mrs. Jones's homeroom in her Social Studies class. Because these students were taught by each of the three fifth grade teachers, I think it was beneficial to observe them as a group in a classroom outside of their homeroom. Students are influenced in varied ways by different people and while I was only able to see this class during their Social Studies instruction, the findings are relevant and valuable to this study.

Again, I was not sure who my participants would be at the time of these classroom observations so I gave careful attention to all students and actions occasionally utilizing Carspecken's (1996) Method of Priority Observation (pp. 48–49). This classroom was set up in the exact opposite of Mrs. Frost's third grade class, so I found a spot in the back of the room, which was right by the door. I was set back about six feet from the back row of the classroom, which periodically made hearing students in the front of the room difficult. Once more, I tried to be as unobtrusive as possible while I watched and took my notes.

The first observation was during a class review of the Battle of Lexington and Concord. To begin, the teacher asked a question, called on a student to answer, and moved on to the next. After which, the class re-read aloud a section in their textbooks about Lexington and Concord. Students round-robin read and the teacher corrected them, during which Mrs. Brooks asked them comprehension questions about what was just read. In my comments, I noted that the kids appeared to be very accustomed to this reading and questioning method. They were all quiet and seemed to be following along. Similar to Mrs. Frost's review lessons, Mrs. Brooks believed that if she taught the material students should have learned it evidenced through sentiments like, "We talked about it three or four times now, every hand should be up." "We just read it." "They should all sound familiar to you" (Mrs. Brooks, personal communication, April 26, 2016).

The lesson continued with the class "doing" their notes, which consisted of Mrs. Brooks asking a question and then writing the responses in bullet points (like, "British General Gage heard that there were weapons stored in Concord") on the whiteboard for students to copy into their notebooks. Next, Mrs. Brooks wrote 9 years between 1763 and 1774 on the board and put up a list of events like "Boston Tea Party." She stated an event and called on a student to give the date, if they were correct, the match was written, if not she prompted the student until he/she figured it out. Again, students were copying this information into their notebooks. This was very quickly paced and the kids were silent as they copied down the information given to them. Before I left, Mrs. Brooks mentioned that it takes an entire quarter of the school year to get through one chapter in Social Studies and that this was the second day the class was working on the same thing, Lexington and Concord. I was surprised at the amount of time devoted to such a limited amount of content.

WHAT THE KIDS HAVE TO SAY

The beginning of my next observation the following day was a vocabulary quiz, there was a list of terms written on the whiteboard, the teacher read aloud a definition and the kids wrote the corresponding word. Students then graded their own work and the papers were handed back to a bin. In my observer comments, I noted the organization of this as well as the other procedures Mrs. Brooks had established with her class. It was almost like watching little robots; the students quietly did everything they were asked very efficiently without disruption or deviation. The next group assignment was filling out a graphic organizer, which Mrs. Brooks had already completed. She asked a student a question and when answered correctly she revealed the response for the class to copy. This time, if a student answered incorrectly Mrs. Brooks quickly moved on to the next student. Perhaps she thought students should know this material as it was a chapter review. Regardless, kids did not seem to be affected positively or negatively if they answered correctly or incorrectly; there was no praise or reprimand.

Homework was assigned (a crossword puzzle worksheet) and threats were given, "In my homeroom the kids had to erase because they rushed to be the first done," "If you miss one it will be an 80, you can't miss one vocab matching, you miss two—60%," and "You need to put effort in, think about your grade on your progress report. How much effort do you want to put into your Social Studies grade at the end of the year?" (Mrs. Brooks, personal communication, May 10, 2016). Here, Mrs. Brooks is using personal consequence as a mechanism of control.

My final observation was ten days later, again during one of these monotonous Social Studies lessons. To begin the class, Mrs. Brooks had the students take out their homework from the night before, five students did not have it done, which meant they received a Homework Notice. "Now we have to wait for these guys" (Mrs. Brooks, personal communication, May 19, 2016). Once the notices were written and those students were exiled to stand in the hallway to wait while Mrs. Brooks went over the homework, matching the name of a person with his description by calling on students for the answers. She seemed annoyed when the students answered incorrectly, "You should know this—we just talked about this" (Mrs. Brooks, personal communication, May 19, 2016). As students turned in this paper, Mrs. Brooks commented to me, "I can't believe the answers I got. I'll just take this home and I'll just guess" (personal communication, May 19, 2016).

Again, the class completed a graphic organizer in the same mechanical fashion. Teacher asked, student answered, everyone wrote. Notably, at the end of the period one student pointed out that the word Confederation was misspelled on Mrs. Brooks' graphic organizer. In an annoyed tone she responded,

"Do I point out your mistakes? Every mistake you make do I point out? Think about that when you're going to point out someone else's mistake" (personal communication, May 19, 2016). This reaction seemed severe to me but I think students are expected to act, work, and behave in fixed ways and this student was resisting Mrs. Brooks' established norms.

It was during this final observation that a theme emerged to me for these fifth grade observations: discipline. The students have been disciplined in various ways to produce automaticity and efficiency in the classroom. This was evidenced in every aspect of what I watched and heard go on in Mrs. Brooks' Social Studies classroom. Students did not deviate from the teacher expectations. On one occasion a student was actually whispering to her neighbor so Mrs. Brooks asked her sharply, "Sue, question?" to which she received no response. Discipline requires consequence and these are noticeable in different ways, here are only a few from my observations: (1) students answered incorrectly and the teacher moved on, (2) homework notices and removal from the classroom, (3) teacher comments that imply if a student does not know something they are at fault or deficient, (4) grades, and (5) getting publically called out for things like, not paying attention, not having materials, talking, etc. While these consequences may not seem very harsh, they assuredly have an effect upon students. It seems as though students have internalized Mrs. Brooks' discipline and can now regulate themselves to act and behave as expected.

Eighth Grade

I approached Mrs. Mackley about participating in my research because we had served on the same committee for a couple of years. She was happy to help me with my study. Mrs. Mackley has been teaching at our district's junior high school for twelve years. The first four of those years were as a sixth grade Language Arts teacher, four more years were spent teaching as the ELL (English Language Learner) Teacher, one year as the seventh grade Social Studies teacher, and two years as an eighth grade Language Arts Teacher. Mrs. Mackley holds an M.A. degree in Curriculum Instruction and an M.A. degree Educational Administration. She has her B.A. degree in Elementary Education and an A.A. degree in General Education. She is certified in Elementary Education (K-9) and Administration. Mrs. Mackley also holds Middle School Endorsements in Reading, Language Arts, Social Science, and English as a Second Language as Mrs. Mackley is fluent in the Polish language.

I began my observations immediately and these took place during the first period of the school day. Mrs. Mackley had her homeroom at the time and following housekeeping items she taught reading. There was an entirely different mood at the junior high school than at the elementary building. I couldn't identify it immediately but as my observations continued and certainly through this analysis, a contrasting (to third and fifth grade) theme emerged. One of the first things I noticed was when the school announcements came on over the PA system, the student announcer recited the Pledge of Allegiance and while all of the students stood, some put their hands on their hearts, and only a few verbally participated.

Following the announcements, Mrs. Mackley explained the day's lesson regarding the themes of the students' books. All of the students had their own personal book to identify a theme or themes that they would like to discuss with their groups. And the kids settled into reading and scribbling on sticky-notes. During this silent reading work time, Mrs. Mackley circulated throughout the room stopping to conference with the students individually. Students were given a two-minute warning that this portion of the lesson was going to be concluding and they would begin "fish-bowling," which was a term I was unfamiliar with but through my observation deduced that students sit around a table and have a discussion. Students then engaged in polite conversation with one another about the themes of their books. Some students asked questions and offered suggestions. I was impressed with their thoughtful interaction but asked in my observer comments, "Are they just going through the motions? They are responding thoughtfully but don't really seem into it? Maybe because it's so early in the day?" It might seem as though the students knew what was expected of them and they were just going along because it was easier than an alternative.

My next observation took place two days later and Mrs. Mackley announced that they were beginning their next fiction unit, to which at least one student rolled her eyes. Students were going to explore some books and make a poster to present to the class. "You know you each have to play a role. I'm not going to tell you what role you have to do but everyone must participate" (Mrs. Mackley, personal communication, May 4, 2016). The kids began shifting at the tables and discussing the book they were given. Some took on leadership roles guiding the conversation while others sat mostly silent. All of the groups were spending a great deal of time on drawing titles and no content about genre, which was the focus of this lesson. It appeared that the meaning of the assignment was lost to the students or perhaps this was a form of their resistance. They were again, superficially completing the task at hand seemingly disinterested in the teacher's intended objective.

During my final day of observation, I noted that Mrs. Mackley was very personal with her students, her interactions with them exuded care. The students came in very excited that one student had gotten in trouble at breakfast for throwing a chair. Mrs. Mackley calmingly said, "Nobody's in trouble—it's okay" (personal communication, May 5, 2016). Following homeroom housekeeping things, the day's reading lesson was about the subgenre of their personal books, "Just a reminder I'm going to ask you what's your subgenre and why" (Mrs. Mackley, personal communication, May 5, 2016). This statement reinforces that Mrs. Mackley wanted her students to be successful and she was not trying to trick or confuse them.

Again, as students read, Mrs. Mackley circulated the room to individually conference with students about their books. The students seemed very comfortable talking to their teacher. There was an ease of conversation and students looked directly at her. Mrs. Mackley was very complimentary and there was a lot of smiling during this conferring. The teacher asked the students personal questions related to their texts and offered personal anecdotes as well. I do not think students are given enough opportunities in school to really have conversations with their teachers and I really enjoyed listening to the kids speak with Mrs. Mackley. That superficial tone previously observed was absent when the students were conversing with their teacher.

These observations were very different than those from the elementary building. Where themes of discipline and obedience emerged with the younger students, themes of autonomy and resistance emerged at the junior high. It is only through a person's independence that one might begin to resist the power and control of an institution. Many points in my observation led me to think that Mrs. Mackley wanted her students to be independent and have choices in their education like allowing the students to read their own books in reading class, allowing them to work in groups but without specified roles, not forcing them to participate in The Pledge of Allegiance every morning, etc. However, these were all "controlled choices" within the accepted grid of school regularities. Nevertheless, students in Mrs. Mackley's class had far more freedoms than those in either Mrs. Jones' or Mrs. Frost's classes. During almost every observation the students went through the motions of the given assignment. They were thoughtful and respectful but their disinterest was apparent. They did what their teacher wanted them to do and said what their teacher wanted them to say. Perhaps this was their form of resistance to the content, assignment, teacher, institution, etc.

The background of these classrooms is intended to give a deeper understanding of the settings from which the students I interviewed had spent their school year. While I only had the opportunity to observe three days in each class, I think valuable insight can be extracted. This will hopefully enrich the understanding of individual student interviews. In the next section, I will briefly discuss each of the seven student participants' central ideas.

Their Big Ideas

In this section, I will introduce the seven participants from my study. While I cannot provide extensive background for each child, I can explain what the students were like during our individual interviews and share their prominent ideas. While all of the interviewees were very accommodating to the questions I posed, they all had their personal focus and I think it is important to have an understanding of these before I share the six common themes of standardized assessment practice in public schools that emerged in this research.

Third Grade
Emily

Emily was a White nine-year-old girl who seemed a bit nervous and reserved to speak with me at the onset of our meeting. She quickly relaxed though, had a snack, and opened up, adding a great deal to the questions I asked and the overall conversation we had. Emily was very animated in her speaking and frequently used hand gestures and air quotes. She had a sense of humor and was generally at ease throughout the interview.

Emily was arguably the student who *wanted* to speak with me the most. She had a lot to say about all of these tests, mostly negative, and she hoped I could do something to stop their prevalence. Over and over, Emily spoke of her anxiety, worry, and nervousness. For example, I asked Emily about the length of testing (seven days):

Emily:	I dreaded it.
Interviewer:	You dreaded it, why?
Emily:	Because I felt like it was never doing to stop. (personal communication, May 11, 2016)

I was both heartbroken and outraged at the sentiments Emily shared regarding her experience.

Being in the classroom and participating in their administration, I had experience with how students engaged with the tests but getting to sit down and hear from Emily what it was like in her own words was very revealing.

Beyond these adverse feelings Emily frequently spoke of the personal consequences attached to these tests. Much of what she had to say was speculation, but these consequences added to her feelings of anxiety. "I was really nervous too and some days in the middle because I felt like if I got it wrong I would get like an F on some grades or something, like something bad would happen" (Emily, personal communication, May 11, 2016). As in this example, Emily was not exactly sure of the consequences attached to the tests but she repeatedly said there were negative outcomes for poor performance on the exams and she felt a great deal of pressure to do well.

Lexie

Lexie was a Hispanic nine-year-old girl who was noticeably comfortable speaking with me. From the start of our interview, there were no signs of nervousness or stress about speaking with an adult one-on-one. She seemed happy to answer my questions and added some interesting comments at the closing of our interview about her family and school lunches, which were clearly unrelated to my purposes but I took to mean Lexie was relaxed and enjoyed our conversation.

Similar to Emily, Lexie spoke of her unfavorable feelings and experience with standardized assessment but certainly not to the same degree. Lexie had a different focus of conversation. She seemed to tell me what she thought I wanted to hear instead of revealing her true perception. For example, Lexie told me she preferred the math portion of the test over the reading. When I asked why she replied, "Because it's funner, there's more work" (personal communication, May 17, 2016). There were several instances where Lexie made comments of this nature and left me wondering if they were truly how she felt or if this is what she thought she should say to a teacher.

Related to these types of responses was Lexie's tendency to brag about her achievements on the tests and in school. To demonstrate here is the first exchange from our interview session:

Interviewer: I want to know how kids feel about that test you had to take
Lexie: I feel nervous
Interviewer: you were nervous
Lexie: but I got good grades. (personal communication, May 17, 2016)

This notion of doing well was echoed throughout our interview as were comments related to outperforming others and being smart. Again, I thought perhaps Lexie was showing-off because she thought I, as a teacher, would be proud of her achievements. And in actuality, I would praise Lexie with a "Wow!" or "Good for you!" when she shared her accomplishments. I felt like she needed the positive recognition and Lexie would return my compliments with a big smile.

Fifth Grade
Chris

Chris was a White eleven-year-old boy who was very articulate and spoke using hand gestures and a slight stutter. He never appeared to be flustered, nervous or confused with what I was asking. Chris seemed very comfortable talking to me and snacked while we carried on our conversation. Chris was very open and seemingly honest in his responses and elaboration.

As with all of the students interviewed, Chris spoke to many of the overarching themes of this research however, his central focus lies within the significance and importance of testing in school. Chris repeatedly verbalized both his agreement with the current testing practices in school and also their necessity. He was certain that these tests were utilized in the students' future and speculated they might be for the junior high, high school, or college. Here is an example from the very beginning of our interview; I asked Chris to tell me what the PARCC was like and he shared that the scores were used when he got older. I then specifically asked how he thought the PARCC scores were used when he was older. "Like to show like for the professors and teachers in the head of the colleges, uh they'll look back at your scores and grades and see what like college you'd fit to go in" (personal communication, May 9, 2016). To Chris, these tests were very important to him as student and his future.

Additionally, Chris spoke to the idea that reading and math were far more important subject areas than subjects like social studies. Interestingly, these are the two areas testing with the PARCC. Further, Chris claimed reading and math have "real life" significance, which is why they need to be targeted the most in school. Chris also thought we should start preparing students to take these tests at much earlier grades than third because they are so important. And that teachers know what is best for their students when it comes to what students have to learn in order to be prepared for their tests. Late in our interview we spoke about Chris' central point.

Interviewer:	So, is the test like the end-all? Is it the most important thing in school?
Chris:	I believe so.
Interviewer:	You do?
Chris:	Yeah. (personal communication, May 9, 2016)

Ideas reflecting the priority Chris places on standardized assessment underlie his entire interview.

Gary

Gary was a White eleven-year-old boy who was very easygoing and seemingly comfortable talking to me. He pleasantly answered any question I posed and really enjoyed speaking to me. Many times, I had to refocus our conversation because Gary wanted to discuss things that interested him. As with my interview with Lexie, I view this off-topic dialogue as a reflection of the students' feelings of ease in speaking with me and/or taking advantage of speaking with an adult who truly wants to hear what they have to say.

When I reviewed Gary's interview, the overarching theme seemed to be related to his laid-back, obedient attitude toward testing and school in general. Many times, when I asked his opinion, he responded with things like, "I was fine with it and didn't have any problems with it" (personal communication, May 12, 2016). Gary's interview revealed his compliance with the many policies, practices, and procedures in school including those of testing, which directly speaks to the theoretical foundation of this research, governmentality.

Gary had a lot to share with me and spoke to many of the overall themes I developed but he mostly spoke in passive terms. Nothing seemed to bother him or really stand out as far as school was concerned. On a few occasions, Gary expressed his interest in Science and Physical Education but added that they had less value than Reading and Math as the latter had more real-life application (and again are the focus of the PARCC test). For example, at the conclusion of Gary's interview he told me he wanted to be a director like George Lucas and an Astronomer,

Interviewer: You are going to be busy. So how do you think your school now is going to affect your future?
Gary: Like adding, of course you have to do that in real life, basically the basic math is just adding, multiplication, subtraction, and division.
Interviewer: So, you think math is the most important stuff you learn in school?
Gary: And subtraction and multiplication/division.
Interviewer: Yeah.
Gary: That's the stuff I'm probably most likely going to use.
Interviewer: So, it's important to you that the stuff you learn in school you can use outside of school?
Gary: Yeah.

Utility of content will be addressed later when I discuss overall themes but here I think this speaks to Gary's docility. He clearly has interest in areas outside of Math and Reading yet he feels compelled to highlight these areas as most important in school.

Eighth Grade
Ana

Ana was a fourteen-year-old Arab girl who was very quiet and reserved throughout our interview. Her teacher regarded her as a thoughtful, respectful, and high achieving student. She seemed a bit nervous speaking to me and frequently would look around the room. Ana gave very short, concise responses to the questions I asked and did not care to elaborate. She was articulate and polite during our conversation.

Ana's two main areas of focus I found are somewhat contradictory in nature (1) apprehension about testing and (2) resistance to testing. To begin, throughout the interview Ana expressed her anxiety about standardized assessments. This idea is illustrated here,

Ana: Well, I'm always nervous.
Interviewer: How come?
Ana: I don't know I'm just a nervous test taker. (personal communication, May 16, 2016)

She repeatedly spoke to the pressure she placed upon herself to do well on these tests. Some of the stress came from school and some came from her parents but mostly from herself. The difficulty of content and format as well as the perceived consequences of these standardized assessments added to Ana's anxiety.

On the other hand, Ana highlighted the insignificance of the PARCC test and I think that speaks to her second important area of focus, resistance. She seemed to go along with the testing because that is what she is supposed to do as an obedient student but lacks any motivation or responsibility to do well. Here is part of our conversation about the MAP (district-wide standardized assessment) compared to the PARCC,

Interviewer: Okay, how does that MAP test compare to the PARCC test?
Ana: There was, I mean, less pressure when I was taking the PARCC test.
Interviewer: Oh okay, how come?
Ana: Um because the MAP test shapes your future and where you're going in life. So yeah, the PARCC test I think was a small part in my future. (personal communication, May 16, 2016)

Ana is not the only student who referred to "going along" with the testing but I think she articulated the most clearly and it became a central area of focus.

Simply doing what they are supposed to can be viewed as a form of resistance when we are exposed to the motivation behind such action. Ana explained that the PARCC test does not matter to her, there was no benefit or consequences, so she just cooperates.

Sal

Sal was a White fourteen-year-old boy who was again regarded by his teacher as a good student and a very nice young man. He was polite and courteous during our interview. Sal did not appear nervous to speak to me and cordially answered all of my questions. Similar to Ana, Sal was quite brief in his responses and did not offer much elaboration. Upon reflection of Sal's interview, I noted themes of purpose kept emerging, which is where I think his personal area of focus lies.

Sal frequently spoke to these tests being used for high school or in high school. "Like I think like it probably would affect you in high school like if you got a really bad grade or like score on it you probably, if you're in honors you'd probably go to the normal" (personal communication, May 20, 2016). Sal spoke to the notion that some of the standardized assessments administered in the junior high school have lasting consequences like in the previous quote. However, he also shares that the scores on the statewide yearly exams, have never affected him. I think these contradictory statements allude to the over-testing practices of public education in our country. Students are constantly assessed in school, which leads to a confusion of which test is for which purpose. They blur the assessments, their requirements, and purposes because they are over-tested, which of course leads to invalid results.

Brooke

Brooke did not come from the participant classroom for this study. Her mother approached me at a school function and asked if I would interview her daughter, as she saw value in the purposes of this study. Through her interview, I learned that Brooke was enrolled in our district's Gifted and Talented Program (GAT) for high achieving students. This program no longer exists in our district. Brooke was a fourteen-year-old White female student who was very open and well spoken. She gave detailed responses to my questions and was polite and caring.

Upon analysis of Brooke's individual interview, I found she frequently spoke about the consequences of standardized assessments. These effects ranged from personal consequences, to teacher consequences, to district consequences. Similar to the conversation I had with Ana regarding the differences between the MAP (district assessment) and the PARCC, Brooke highlighted personal consequence,

Brooke: How are they the same, well in different ways they are because they're testing and it's for the state and it's affecting you in some way but like it's different because for me it effects on where I'm placed in high school and so
Interviewer: Which one does, the MAP or the PARCC?
Brooke: I'm sorry, the MAP, yeah that affects where I'm placed in high school so I like have to try, really have to try if I want to get into a good class in high school. Where like PARCC it doesn't really affect where I'm going.

Brooke also mentioned personal consequences of these tests affecting her future career opportunities.

Beyond personal effects were the consequences these tests have upon teachers. Brooke noted that the PARCC test specifically is to see how well the teachers are teaching, which is directly linked to district consequences involving funding. Brooke reports that both teachers and her building principal stressed the significance of the PARCC test as it is tied to funding of the school. She was motivated to do well because "I feel like it will affect the school and I have a sibling that's going to be going to that school and I don't want it to be like a horrible school because I didn't try my best on the PARCC test" (personal communication, May 26, 2016). As previously discussed, our state relies heavily upon federal funding, which is linked to student performance on the PARCC test. Brooke is clearly concerned with the consequences of student achievement on standardized tests and I found that to be her main area of focus in her interview.

CHAPTER 7

Interpreting Student Voice: Themes

> *The very language you use in your description is likely to be saturated with values, frequently your own. No descriptive discourse is, or can be, value-free; advocacy or interpretation is thus, to some degree and inevitably, part of your account.*
>
> FIELDING (2004, P. 297)

∴

Six common themes of standardized assessment practice in public schools that emerged in this research include: (1) adverse attitudes, feelings, and experiences with testing practices, (2) purposes and consequences of standardized assessments, (3) the ways that standardized tests are used to normalize through labeling and sorting student populations, (4) the ways in which students exhibit obedience, (5) student references to a hierarchy of power and control in schools, and (6) technologies of the self.

I am very clear in my role as a student voice researcher. I understand that while I have let the students speak for themselves, ultimately I am choosing what to include and what to leave out of this study. As Margaret LeCompte (1993) reminds us, "The discourse selected may be powerful, truthful, and authentic but it is, in fact, still partial discourse…(which) often leaves the researcher, as an absent presence" (as quoted in Fielding, 2004, p. 299). As previously discussed, my personal experience, bias, and purposes play a role in my interpretation of the data. I have given every effort to convey the students' thoughts and ideas in truthful and meaningful ways throughout this study.

In the coming section I will break each theme into its own subsection in an effort to provide us with insights into testing practices in public schools today and how students are governed, manipulated, and controlled through the standardization process. The common themes I developed are informed by governmentality and student voice literature and build upon the literature through the experiences of seven public school children.

Adverse Attitudes, Feelings, and Experiences with Testing Practices

Every student in this research study articulated adverse or negative attitudes, feelings, and experiences with standardized assessment practices in school. These feelings generally spanned areas of confusion, disgust, and difficulty of content, format, and/or material. Additionally, concerns with time were quite prevalent as were references to lack of preparation. Minarechová (2012) reports that students experience a wide-range of impacts manifested in various forms such as,

> Stress and tension in students, teachers' preferences for "better" students, undermining of student self-esteem and in some cases even student fear of failure and the associated consequences. The students suffer in various psychological and physical ways, for example, anxiety, stress, exhaustion resulting from lack of food and water, an increase in blood pressure and the rate of respiration, elevated body temperature, gastrointestinal problems, headaches, difficulty sleeping, and muscle spasms. (p. 91)

With the enormous amount of negative effects resulting from tests of this nature, it is not surprising that the students in this research study present negative feelings toward them.

Nervousness was the most prevalent adverse feeling toward testing that the participants expressed. Five out of seven of the students reported feeling nervous to some degree. The third grade students, Emily and Lexie, spoke about their anxiety the most. These girls referred to the PARCC test as being scary and they were nervous because they had never experienced an assessment in this capacity. I can corroborate their sentiment, as a third grade teacher for eight years, I have witnessed students participate in this test for the first time. Their anxiety and stress is tremendous, many years I have had students report feeling sick, afraid, and confused. But third graders were not alone in feeling nervous about these tests. Chris, Ana, and Brooke all shared the same apprehension regarding the PARCC test. As Ana affirms, "I was nervous, ya' know everyone's nervous" (personal communication, May 16, 2016). It certainly seems that to some extent all of the students I interviewed shared Ana's sentiment, whether they used the word nervous in their statements or not.

Confusion is another aspect students frequently described throughout the interviews. As I previously discussed, the PARCC test is notoriously confusing. One of the many issues plaguing the PARCC test is that it consists largely of objective format items; multiple-choice and Evidence Based Selected Response (EBSR) items. Shepherd (2014) explains, "These item types are most appropriate for testing very low-level skills (e.g. recall or factual detail)." However, on the PARCC test these questions are used to test higher-order thinking, which makes them convoluted and ambiguous. Referring to parcconline.org (2015), EBSR "combines a traditional selected-response question that asks students to show evidence from the test that supports the answer they provided to the first question." The trouble is that the questions are supposed to deal with high-order thinking skills and the wrong answers are all supposed to be reasonable, so the test questions end up being extremely complicated and tricky. For many of the questions, no one answer choice is more correct than the others or the question simply is not answerable as written (Shepherd, 2014). This is a very confusing test as the students I interviewed stated many times.

Again, five out of the seven students specifically stated that the test was in fact, confusing. Brooke explicitly identifies EBSR questions as a point of confusion,

> I thought they were kind of confusing because there were answers and they would go along with like there was a Part A and Part B. And it would go along with Part A but then there were like separate answers that would go along too so it was kind of confusing on which one goes with which answer. So I thought that was confusing. (personal communication, May 26, 2016)

Unfortunately, in an effort to develop a complex test, it appears as though, the creators of the PARCC test sought to confuse children as the one way to make the test difficult. As Brooke articulated it's a messy format that students have a hard time working with.

Students point out their confusion in other areas of the PARCC test as well. Like Sal, in reference to another aspect of the English Language Arts portion, "I didn't like the essay part because sometimes I didn't understand what it was like asking for you to write" (personal communication, May 20, 2016) Or Gary describing the Math portion, "I didn't know what to do with the problems sometimes" (personal communication, May 12, 2016). The subjective-referenced truth claim I am making here is that students find the PARCC test confusing for a variety of reasons based upon their given statements.

Additionally, students voiced their thoughts regarding the difficulty of both the content and format of the PARCC test. Not surprising, the third grade students spoke to the greatest extent regarding the complications they had with the test. I can corroborate their concerns as I have administered the state test to third grade students for years. My students have reported feeling sick, scared, worried, and confused during their first experience with the state test. Both Lexie and Emily exaggerated the level and complexity of certain math questions that were posed on the test. Additionally, both girls described extremely difficult language and terminology used in PARCC test questions. Here is how a nine-year-old perceived a few of the questions on the PARCC test,

Emily: One of the questions were in German, it was all in German and I couldn't even read that question, what it was telling me to do. And then I had another one that was in like Dutch or something.
Interviewer: What? That's wild; did you tell your teacher?
Emily: Yeah and she said I can't help you, just try your best. (personal communication, May 11, 2016)

At first glance Emily's statements seem rather comical; of course, the test was not written in German or Dutch. But realistically speaking, if a capable, English-speaking student cannot understand the words and language utilized, that says a great deal about the difficulty and accessibility of the content on the PARCC test.

Similarly, Ana and Chris both stated that there were questions addressing skills and content that they had not learned. Beyond difficult content, there were several documented issues with the formatting of the PARCC test. For example, when I was speaking to Ana about the Math portion of the PARCC test she mentioned that the extended response questions were difficult because, "it's like you only know how to do the work, not to explain it" (personal communication, May 16, 2017). In these types of questions students are required to solve a math problem then explain their thinking through a typed response. Perhaps, Ana's difficulty lies in a lack of experience, practice, or teaching but more likely the demanding and cumbersome task of documenting exactly what she did and why she did it is to blame.

With regard to format, the PARCC test lacks any valid, reasonable, or logical measures. To begin, the test is intended to be administered through a computer-based method, which requires each child to be logged onto a given website simultaneously. For most elementary-age children, this test becomes one of keyboarding skills and computer experience, rather than assessment in ELA or mathematics. Students from low-income homes, who do not have electronic devices (especially computers) will inevitably score much lower on assessments administered in such manner. Consequently, it seems that the PARCC would certainly not have the ability to measure achievement in an equitable way and that at best it would only be able to accurately measure social stratification. Furthermore, the ELA format requires students to flip (screens or pages) between two or more passages to answer "comprehension" questions and write an essay, which becomes very difficult and demanding for a child.

The computer format was an area of concern for the students I interviewed. Gary, Ana, and Brooke all noted that a student's typing skills are a factor in both test achievement and completion. Brooke said, "I feel like the time is too short because especially now on the laptops you have to type everything out" (personal communication, May 26, 2016). Time is the next area of concern the students addressed during our interviews. Five out of eight of the participants, across all three grade levels spoke to the issue of time.

As administrators of the PARCC test, classroom teachers are required to read directions from a script. Within this script are time limits for each testing session, teachers then tell their students how many minutes they have to complete the test, when there are ten minutes remaining, and when their time has expired. This procedure alone was stressful for Emily, she reported that the teacher kept telling her how many minutes there were and that the questions were very long. Lengthy reading passages and written responses take the students a great deal of time to complete.

Emily stated that when she was reading the stories and writing the essays, she felt like she would not finish. Brooke agreed, "When I started to run out of time I just started to like hurry up and put down as much as I could" (personal communication, May 26, 2016). But Emily did not rush through, she actually ran out of time and did not complete one of these ELA testing sessions. When that happens, teachers simply log the student out because the time has expired. Ana also mentioned that some students in her class were not able to complete the tests because they ran out of time. On the other hand, Chris never felt like he was short on time, "It felt like a long time...I was sitting there looking up at the clock like, "when is this gonna be over?"' (personal communication, May 9, 2016). Regardless of whether the time seemed limited or extended, the normative-evaluative truth claim I am making based upon this data is that time parameters for testing sessions is not preferable and results in adverse student reactions and feelings.

Students in grades three and five participated in four Math testing sessions and three ELA testing sessions, resulting in seven school days of PARCC testing. The students in eighth grade participated in three Math testing sessions and three ELA testing sessions, resulting in six days of PARCC testing. When I asked Lexie about taking the tests for seven days, she responded that she hated it because it was so many days. Similarly, Gary felt that the length of days felt very long.

A final area of testing to which the students attached a negative connotation lies in preparation practices in school. Prior to conducting these student interviews, I held the assumption that students would likely view the time teachers spent on preparation work for the PARCC test as unfavorable; my hypothesis was incorrect. To the contrary, five of the students I interviewed reported that they would have either liked more preparation practice, began preparing at a younger age, and if they were the teachers they would have given their students more PARCC practice to get them ready.

Both Lexie and Gary voiced their concerns of being unprepared for portions of the test and that occasionally there were items on the test that they had not learned yet. Further, Lexie mentioned she would have liked more practice to know more about how to use the computers. Chris would like to see test preparation begin at a younger age:

> I would believe all of them [tests] are highly important to every single child and I think some second and first graders and maybe some kindergarten, they should be able to take the test if they want to. And if they do bad at it they could choose either to put it as their future or erase it from their papers if they're younger and they did poorly...so they're prepared for the future when it actually does count for them and their future. (personal communication, May 9, 2015)

Chris' statements are indicative of both the importance he places upon standardized testing and his desire to do well on such assessments.

Minarechová (2012) explains that gifted and talented students are negatively affected by high-stakes testing manifested as boredom, or frustration and anger because of the slow pace of teaching, the disproportionate amount of time spent on test preparation and the constant repetition of basic skills (p. 90). Emily spoke to these ideas in her interview,

> We've spent two or three months on learning just the angles and some kids, like there's only like three kids that don't know all the angles. But most kids know everything and they're stuck in the classroom for thirty-five minutes learning about it all over and that's kind of boring...I think she [the teacher] wants everybody to learn, *everybody* to be at the same level but those kids are never [stops abruptly before continuing] like they're gonna take so long to get on the level and we're gonna be higher than them. (personal communication, May 11, 2016)

Emily's statements can certainly be viewed as insensitive to the needs of her peers but they can also be reflective of the monotonous, futile, and uninteresting practice of standardized testing preparation in the classroom.

Finally, I asked students what they would do if they were the teachers when it came to all of this testing. Most said they would do what their teachers had done and a few indicated that they would have given their students more practice if they were in charge. Sal would have his students start taking practice tests at the beginning of the school year so the students could see how they would do. Emily would tell her students if they were doing something in their math or writing lessons that "this would be on the test or something like this would be on the test" (personal communication, May 11, 2015). She felt like if her teacher had told her what was going to be on the test she would have an easier time when the PARCC test became a reality.

Brooke explained that some of her Math and Language Arts teachers gave the students PARCC practice packets as preparation for the test. She noted that these helped take some of her stress and anxiety away because she had an idea of what was going to be on the test. However, she also spoke to the uncertainty of the PARCC test and I think her insight is significant to the purposes of this study. "Well, you don't really know what's coming on the test so it's kind of like you can practice as much as you want but it doesn't mean you're going to get what's on the test so it doesn't really matter how much practice you get (personal communication, May 26, 2016). I think Brooke's statement speaks to the ambiguity of the PARCC test as well as the students' adverse feelings, reactions, and experiences with the test.

Purposes and Consequences of Standardized Assessments

As I coded my student data, I separated the areas of purposes of standardized testing and consequences, however these categories certainly overlap as the coming section will show. Students in this research study identified personal consequences as the most prevalent, followed by teacher consequences, and finally school or district consequences. Additionally, student interview data revealed the purposes of standardized testing as the utility of content and teacher instruction. This theme directly relates to the following research questions guiding this study: how do students understand the purpose of testing, what is/are the function(s) of testing, are there personal, school-wide, district-wide, state-wide, etc. benefits or consequences and how do students perceive the impact or lack thereof?

Every student interviewed spoke to the idea that standardized tests have personal consequences. The effects the students voiced mostly centered around grades and placement. Three of the seven students believed that the PARCC test was somehow used to influence their report card grades. Lexie articulated this notion, "Your score is like for a grade. Like if we're doing on the PARCC tests if there was a math, like it will probably go on our math grade" (personal communication, May 17, 2016). While this is likely not the case as teachers typically do not receive state testing results for their students until the following school year, the fear for the kids can be very real. Emily explains, "I put lots of pressure on myself because I thought like it would be really bad if I got a bad grade on something even if I didn't know it" (personal communication, May 11, 2016). Again, the youngest students in this study spoke the most about the PARCC test being graded and affecting their grades in school. They are inexperienced with the testing, scoring procedures, and consequences. Chris also noted that the PARCC scores could be used for grades or future placement in school.

Five of the seven participants identified future placement as a personal consequence of high stakes testing. This conversation expanded from solely the PARCC test and often students voiced their concerns with the district-wide standardized assessment measure, the MAP test, as well. The subject of placement ranged from classroom assignment in the elementary school, to placement in junior high school, to high school, and even college. To begin, Emily explained that she has always thought that certain classroom teachers have specific students in their classes based upon their achievement. In the elementary building, there are three classrooms at each grade level. Emily says, "I always thought this; some teachers teach the below average kids and some teachers teach the high average, and some teachers teach the average and I think they [PARCC scores] would determine what teachers you would have because of the records" (personal communication, May 11, 2016). As a school, students are not tracked based on their ability. However, at the time of this study students in grades three through five were ability-grouped for their reading instruction. Students are no longer tracked for reading but students in grades four and five continue to be ability grouped for mathematics instruction.

The students in fifth grade spoke mostly about standardized test scores being responsible for their placement in junior high school. Chris stated that the scores would determine, "who would be the best homeroom teacher, math, reading, social studies, and all those other subjects" (personal communication, May 9, 2016). Similarly, Gary believed his scores were going to be used by his sixth grade teachers. Neither fifth grade student was worried that his scores would have a negative effect on his placement, both identified themselves as above average or average. So, I asked Chris what about the students who did poorly on the PARCC test, how would they be affected? Chris replied, "The teachers might not see them as good as they really are" (personal communication, May 9, 2016). This quote speaks volumes. Chris was never concerned with his test scores, and likely does not have to be. Chris is a White, working-class student from a two-parent home; these tests were written for students like him. But what Chris said here is very powerful and true. Too often standardized test scores are used as a means to an end, with very harsh consequences attached to poor performance. Students have come to be viewed as points in a data set, rather than unique individuals and are likely not seen "as good as they really are" because they do not perfectly fit into the standards and expectations set by public schools.

Beyond junior high, the students in this study thought that their scores on standardized tests would impact both their placement in high school and college. All three eighth grade students noted that the MAP test determined their placement in high school as in whether they would be in remedial, average, or honors classes. Ana explains, "That test [MAP] kinda like determined my classes in high school so I thought that was also pretty important" (personal communication, May 16, 2016). As will be discussed in a later section, students in the eighth grade were well aware that the PARCC test did not affect their placement in high school nor were there any other personal consequences.

Again, both fifth grade students noted that they thought the PARCC test scores were likely used for placement in college, as in determining which colleges a student would have the opportunity to attend. On several occasions during the individual interview, Chris noted "PARCC testing is for college" (personal communication, May 9, 2016). He believed that professors and deans would look back at a student's PARCC scores to see if one would "fit" the school. According to parcconline.org, thankfully only five institutions and systems of higher education have policies that formally guide the incorporation of the PARCC assessments into their placement policies and practices. One of these colleges is in our state but assuredly, they are not examining the students' fifth grade PARCC scores. Perhaps the participants in this study believe the scores are used for college because they are not exactly sure, but feel that their scores must hold some significance because of the rigorous and stringent process of PARCC testing.

In addition to personal consequences, four of the students in this study identified teacher, school, and district ramifications based upon students' PARCC test scores. These students thought that their PARCC scores were to determine if the teachers were doing their jobs. Many students cited their own teachers as the source of this belief. "She [my teacher] said it [PARCC test] determined how well the teachers were doing here" (Ana, personal communication, May 16, 2016). Additionally, the students thought that their scores would tell the teachers if they need to improve their teaching or continue to do what they were doing in the classroom. Gary went so far as to speculate that if a teacher's students performed poorly on the PARCC test that teacher would likely be called into the principal's office to be reprimanded. Thankfully, students' achievement on state tests have never been used to rate, chastise, or negatively impact teachers in our school. Leistyna (2007) states that "under extreme pressure to produce results or face losing their jobs, cuts in federal resources, and school closure, educators often lower standards and engage in unethical behavior in order to raise test scores (p. 60). As I briefly mentioned in my introduction, the tides have been turning in our district and the pressure to raise PARCC scores has been increasing. I hope our teachers never reach these desperate levels Leistyna describes and it is truly disheartening to know that educators across the country face these real consequences based upon their students' performance on standardized testing measures.

Only Brooke mentioned the school and district as being affected by students' scores on the PARCC test. She explained that her teachers told the students that, while they were likely not personally affected by their scores on the PARCC test, other things would be affected. Brooke thought that if the students did poorly on the exam the schools would have negative effects. "Our principal would go like, 'This is for the state and its funding.' And the teachers did say not to just slack off and put whatever you want because it does fund the school and it helps the school" (personal communication, May 26, 2016). Brooke mentioned that the PARCC test scores determined the schools' funding and if the students performed poorly some monies would be taken away. She was concerned with this idea and was motivated to do well because her little sister was still in the district and she wanted her to have nice schools. Glasser (1993) speaks to this idea as he termed machine-scored state tests like the PARCC "real-world nonsense" and advised teachers to explain to their students that they may be required to "learn useless material" for their schools to get state funding (p. 82 as cited in Jolley). While it appears as though Brooke's principal and teachers emphasized the connection between the PARCC and district funding, it does not seem like they mentioned the narrow and arbitrary nature of the test itself.

In addition to the aforementioned consequences of standardized testing, four of the students in this study identified the purposes of the PARCC test as utility of content and teacher instruction. By utility I am referring to the notion that students viewed the content as favorable and useful. For example, Brooke, Gary, and Chris explained that English Language Arts and Math are "your top subjects" and are "really important" (Brooke, Gary, personal communication, May 26, May 24, 2016). They thought that these subjects were tested because the skills were critical to the students' future. Participants concluded that the content tested through the PARCC test was useful for their future employment and life in general. Ana noted that these tests were "to get you ready for life… by preparing you, teaching you stuff you will use in your future" (personal communication, May 16, 2016). Similarly, Brooke stated, "You need to know that math is in everything and reading and language arts, you need to know proper English. If you're gonna go off in life you need to, like for a career, you need to know your proper English and Math" (personal communication, May 26, 2016).

These students have been governed in ways that make them believe reading and math are the most important parts of an education. These are the areas that have been focused upon in school, they are the only areas tested by this Midwestern state, and consequently have subjugated other facets of education and alternative views of intelligence. Turnipseed and Darling-Hammond (2015) state, "Our education system undermines the development of higher-order thinking skills by its dogged focus on multiple-choice tests, which discourage critical and creative thinking, as the ultimate measure of student achievement and teacher and school accountability" (p. 2). The normative-evaluative truth claim I am making is that the narrowing of school curriculum has negatively impacted students because it has fostered the belief that ELA and Math are the most important areas of school based upon the given statements from the students in this study.

Finally, three of the seven students mentioned that their performance on the PARCC test was used to assist teachers with instruction. Chris stated, "Like if we're doing bad on it [PARCC test] they [teachers] know what to teach us. If we're doing good they know to teach us a little less of that" (personal communication, May 24, 2016). Ideally, assessments should be utilized by educators to guide instruction. Too often, as is the case with the PARCC test, assessments are used to evaluate and judge. As previously mentioned, the PARCC test does not likely influence teacher instruction as the scores are received the school year following administration. There are cases where teachers use the tests to teach their students the content and strategies to increase their chances of better scores. In their 2007 study, Jones and Egley found that "Many teachers indicated that Florida's testing program has impeded student learning by negatively affecting their teaching practices and forcing them to teach in ways that promote test-taking skills over learning for understanding" (p. 245). This notion is likely echoed across the United States and certainly in our school district. Teachers are not utilizing PARCC scores to help guide their instruction in meaningful ways, if anything they are using the scores to teach their new students how to do better on the test the next year.

Standardized Tests as a Means to Normalize Student Populations

As referred to in Chapter 4, Foucault's theory of governmentality spans both disciplinary and regulatory mechanisms of control. In the seventeenth and eighteenth centuries disciplinary mechanisms of control were solely concentrated on the individual and the body. As such, an effective incorporation of power had to be able to access individuals' acts, attitudes, and modes of everyday behavior. "Hence the significance of methods like school discipline, which succeeded in making children's bodies the object of highly complex systems of manipulation and conditioning (Foucault, 1980, p. 125). Systems of control began to shift at the end of the eighteenth century from considering "man as body" to "man as species." While these control mechanisms are not mutually exclusive, the ideas of regularization and normalization characteristic of Foucault's biopower are the foundation upon which I built the current theme.

Foucault's theory of governmentality introduces the notion of biopolitics in his 1975–76 Lectures at the Collège de France, *Society Must Be Defended.* According to Foucault, biopolitics emerged at the end of the eighteenth century as power and control shifted to managing humans as populations. It is the identification and intervention of phenomena and the construction of populations as political problems (Foucault, 1997, p. 243). It is at this time the first demographers began measuring human phenomena in statistical terms. While Foucault describes the foundations of biopolitical phenomena as birth rate, fertility, death, and illness, efforts to centralize power and normalize knowledge encompass much more of the human experience now (Foucault, 1997, p. 244).

Foucault's biopolitics introduces mechanisms of control including forecasts, statistical estimates, and overall measures. Their purpose is to "intervene at the level at which these general phenomena are determined...regulatory mechanisms must be established to establish an equilibrium, maintain an average...so as to optimize state life" (Foucault, 1997, p. 246). This concept differs from earlier pastoral mechanisms of control insofar as previously humans were viewed as individuals and each person's well-being was ensured by the welfare state. Contrastingly, in the biopolitical milieu the entire population must be balanced and regularized, meaning that some will prosper and others will deteriorate. In terms of standardized assessment, Foucault's equilibrium can be illustrated through a bell curve. According to Investopedia.com (n.d.)

> The bell curve is the most common type of distribution for a variable, and due to this fact, it is known as a normal distribution. The term "bell curve" comes from the fact that the graph used to depict a normal distribution consists of a bell-shaped line. The highest point on the curve, or the top of the bell, represents the most probable event in a series of data, while all other possible occurrences are equally distributed around the most probable event, creating a downward-sloping line on each side of the peak.

Standardized assessments used in schools operate with the bell curve and its "normal" distribution. As Foucault's theory suggests, student scores should fall equally in this type of distribution; a balanced number of students should perform above average and below.

Beyond maintaining an average, Foucault's biopolitical mechanisms take control of the population and ensure that they are "not disciplined, but regularized" (Foucault, 1997, pp. 246–247). It is this notion of normalization through regulatory measures which the participants in this study voiced in their interviews. Students exemplified this theory when they compared themselves to their peers, identified where they performed academically in terms of the bell curve (below-average, average, above-average), and spoke to how this performance would sort or rank them into specific classes. Every student in this study discussed issues I thematically organized as biopolitically normalizing.

PARCC is a mechanism that exhibits the characteristics of normalization, Smith (2015) explains how the test is used for these means,

> ACT and PARCC are standardized assessments that are inaccessible to most students, using text that is too complex and requiring a level of cognition that is completely inappropriate. They are designed as a filter and used to skim the "cream" off the top of the bell-shaped curve. Students who fall into the category of "cream" are admitted into the best colleges and are eligible for scholarships based on their "academic merits". (p. 43)

As students are sorted and labeled, their futures are determined based upon narrow standardized testing measures. Because students are held to universal norms they are regularized and controlled through administration and participation in tests like the PARCC.

Stecher (2002) explains that high-stakes testing has negative effects on students, one such effect is that the tests themselves make students more competitive (as cited in Minarechova, p. 94). Competition has replaced cooperation in many public school classrooms. Both Lexie and Gary specifically named peers in their classrooms to illustrate their own superiority. Lexie noted that a peer in her class only writes three words and calls it a sentence, but Lexie herself writes ten words in a sentence. Similarly, Gary said that when he was on question 10 of the PARCC test a peer was only on question 2 because the other student was always very slow. These students seemingly compared themselves to others to establish their achievement as higher or better than their peers.

The majority of students in this study spoke specifically to their academic standing in terms of below-average, average, or above average and how these identifications impact placement in specific classes or schools. Emily speculated that the state and government makes the students take the PARCC test "because they really want to figure out of you are above average, if you're average, or if you're below average and it seems like they want to pressurize you to find that out" (personal communication, May 11, 2016). This classification through standardized testing measures is characteristic of normalization. Yapa (2011) contends, "Institutions and their discursive practices are the agents by which subjects are divided, classified, and subjected to normalization" (as cited in Batters, p. 9). Discourse in public education systems is not strictly limited to the dominant narratives about school; the materials, curriculum, and of course assessments are part of these discursive practices as well.

Many of the other interviewees used these categorical labels. For example, Chris noted that he "did, well, better than average" and Sal said, "I think I'm above average" during conversations about both the MAP and PARCC tests. As Foucault's theory suggests, the students' performance on these standardized testing measures sorts them into specific tracks of classes in schools. During the fifth grade joint interview, Gary and Chris discussed how students are grouped for math instruction in our school. Here is an excerpt of their conversation,

Gary:	Like there's a low, middle, high. I'm middle, luckily I'm not low.
Chris:	Well, there's no ranking for low, medium, high. It's just some of the classes move on quicker than others.
Gary:	Well, yeah cause Ms. Kashi's class, most of them are really smart, like I'm not the smartest person. Yeah, like I'm like a nerd but not a nerd. I'm like a
Interviewer:	[interrupts] What does that mean?
Gary:	Well
Chris:	Like he isn't too smart and he's not dumb
Gary:	because like I'm
Chris:	he's just normal. (personal communication, May 24, 2016)

According to both Gary and Chris, Gary is average, normal. These boys appear to have been conditioned by the structures of school that sort and rank students. This seems to have become an expected, accepted, and inevitable part of what it means to be a student in public education.

The three eighth grade students in this study all explained that their achievement on standardized tests determined where and how they would be placed in high school. In this way, assessments like the MAP and PARCC test are a means through which students are regularized based upon given standards. When I asked Ana what she thought her PARCC scores might be used for she stated, "Maybe to classify what class you should be in...I think if you get like a score of this or higher they kinda just put you under the list for honors or something" (personal communication, May 16, 2016). While these students may be speculating based on what they think or may have heard, they are accurate in their conjecture. Their placement, as far as which types of classes they are able to enroll in high school are partially and significantly influenced by their performance on the eighth grade standardized tests in which they participate.

The Ways in Which Students Exhibit Obedience

Upon entering a school, we would expect to find children quietly working at their own desks in classrooms segregated by grade level or ability, walking down hallways in single file lines, raising their hands to answer questions, listening and obeying their teachers' directions. This uniformity and creation of docile bodies is one of the greatest detriments that educational institutions have contributed to the formation of a self by children. Students are trained at an early school age, that their behavior must be one of docility, receptivity, and obedience (Dewey, 1938, p. 18). In these institutions, there can be no room for noise, creativity, questions, or straying from the teacher-directed instruction and schedule. Foucault (1995) explains that discipline creates docile bodies so that individuals in power have control, including how others operate with predetermined speed and efficiency (p. 138). The goal of many teachers is to have a quiet classroom running smoothly, free from distraction, in order to get through the material they are supposed to cover that day, week, month, or school year.

Students exhibit obedience when they are docile, "A body is docile that may be subjected, used, transformed, and improved" (Foucault, 1995, p. 136). This section highlights the ways that the students in this study exhibit their docility and obedience with regard to standardized assessments. Children have been trained, disciplined, and surveilled into their obedient and submissive role as students in public education. Six of the seven participants exemplified their compliance with standardized assessments as an inevitable part of school. Additionally, five of the seven interviewees spoke to the idea that the "teacher knows best" as a representation of their submissive role the classroom.

The most common way that students articulated their compliance with standardized testing was their passive opinion toward them. For example, Gary noted, "I was fine with it and I didn't have any problems with it" (personal communication, May 12, 2016). The students seemed indifferent about the tests, for the most part. There were many instances throughout the interviews when students did voice their clear opinions on matters involving assessments but when it came down to their participation, most were okay with it. They have come to view these assessments as part of what being a student means and do not appear to give much thought to why or what their participation means. Ana illustrated this idea when she stated, "I mean I guess they have a purpose and they're important. So, I mean if something's important then I just do it" (personal communication, May 16, 2016). Children in schools are told repeatedly throughout their years as students to do what they are told, to follow directions, and not to pushback. They have not learned to question the motives and purposes of education and their corresponding assessments and therefore do not do so. Foucault (1995) explains that bodies can be disciplined into docility and once docile they can more easily be controlled (pp. 136–137). The students in this study personify this theory through their statements of compliance and obedience.

The two youngest participants, noted that over the seven days of testing they simply got used to it. For third grade students, this is their first experience with statewide standardized testing and both participants had very strong adverse opinions toward their participation. However, Lexie reported, "They both [Reading and Mathematics testing sessions] were kind of hard in the beginning but like after a couple days when you do both, like you get kind of used to it" and Emily agreed, "I kind of got used to it by the last day" (personal communication, May 17, 2016; May 11, 2016). The subjective-referenced truth claim I am making here is that the third grade students are at the beginning of their standardized testing careers in public education and are already demonstrating how they have been governed to accept these assessments, evidenced by the aforementioned statements.

Brooke also voiced her conditioning to standardized tests. When I asked her what she thought about the length (number of days) that the PARCC test took up she responded, "Well, in the beginning I was like, I felt more stressed because I felt like I had a lot to do but as the days went by it got easier because you knew you were almost done" (personal communication, May 26, 2016). While Brooke is in eighth grade and has five years' experience with the yearly statewide standardized test she felt the same as the third grade students. After days of participating in similar testing sessions they all get used to it. Additionally, Brooke spoke to the new (2 years ago) adoption of the PARCC test replacing the Illinois Standards Achievement Test (ISAT). The ISAT had been the statewide test since the year 2000, as Brooke is fourteen years old, up until two years ago this was the only high-stakes exam she had ever taken (CPRE, 2000, p. 1). In a statement she made regarding the transition from the ISAT to the PARCC, Brooke again demonstrated her compliance,

> I feel like when I took like the ISAT I was used to it because I've grown up taking ISAT. So, I was like, "okay, another ISAT test, I'll be fine." But like when PARCC came in I was like, "Oh, my god! This is a brand new test." And it was just a little more stressful cause I didn't, I had no idea what this PARCC test was. (personal communication, May 26, 2016)

Brooke's participation in the ISAT since third grade, as well as many other supporting factors from school itself, have contributed to her docile and impartial attitude and feeling toward the assessment and participation in the assessment. However, the introduction of the PARCC test brought upon feelings of anxiety related to the uncertainty. It is likely that as the years this state continues to mandate the PARCC test as its statewide measure of student achievement, Brooke and her peers will again become "used to" the test.

Another prominent way that students demonstrated their obedience was when they referred to the teacher as knowing what is best for them. These types of statements carry strong submissive and docile undertones. During the individual interviews, there were different times with different students when I would ask what they would do if they were the teachers. Sal, Emily, and Gary all stated that they would do exactly what their teacher had done, whether we were talking about test preparation, or what they got to learn in class. Chris said, "Well, what I think is that whatever the teachers choose would be for the better good for us" (personal communication, May 9, 2016). These students' agreement with their teachers' methods and materials is indicative of their docious role in school. Because there is either no choice or superficial choice in school these students have come to accept their receptive role in the classroom. Demonstrated by the above sentiments, teachers are the keepers on knowledge and assuredly know what is best for their students.

During the student interviews, I questioned the participants about the choices they have in school, every response was either very little choice or no choice at all. When I asked students to explain what they meant by very little choice I would get responses involving what I call, controlled choice. For example, Lexie said that her teacher let the class vote on which Science chapter they would like to study at the end of the school year. Or Sal said that his teacher would let the class vote on whether to take a multiple-choice or short answer test. These choices that the teachers are allowing their students to make are controlled because they must fall within the accepted parameters. These are superficial choices; the kids don't really have a choice. A choice means having an opinion, getting to think for oneself and letting students pick what kind of test they take is not really a "choice."

Emily, Brooke, and Ana all stated that they had no choice in school when it comes to what they learn, how they learn it, or what they can or cannot do in school. I think the exchange Ana and I have regarding choice is beneficial to examine at length:

Interviewer: So, how much choice do you get in what you learn in school.
Ana: No choice at all.
Interviewer: So, why do you think that is?
Ana: Because I don't know stuff, I don't know if I'm going to use it in the future. It's up to my teachers.
Interviewer: So, do you think your teachers know what you're going to need to know in the future?
Ana: Yeah from their experience.
Interviewer: How about your parents do they have any influence over what you learn in school?
Ana: No.
Interviewer: Okay, alright so you don't and your parents don't, do you think you should have a say in what you learn?
Ana: No
Interviewer: How come?
Ana: Because like I said, I don't know any better.

As an advocate for children and student voice work, Ana's statements here are very discouraging. They are also reflective of not only obedience and docility but a lack of autonomy and self-confidence. The students in this study demonstrate the ways in which the reaches of Foucault's governmentality have influenced who they are in relation to school as well as standardized testing and their compliance is just one of those examples.

Student References to a Hierarchy of Power and Control in Schools

In Dean's (2010) description of Foucault's notion of government, he explains that government "involves a form of power over others that is made operable through the liberties of those over whom it is exercised" (p. 58). Only when the population accepts the terms and actions of a government does it have any power. This is a founding principle of Foucault's theory of governmentality; individuals are manipulated and controlled by governmental bodies to comply with such exercises of power as just and inevitable. Students in this study referred to a hierarchy of control within educational institutions regarding standardized assessment measures. Additionally, six out of the seven participants made specific mention of the state or national government as playing a role in public education.

Every student in this study spoke about the ways that a hierarchy of power controls what is taught and what students learn in school. Lexie very clearly articulated a form of this hierarchy I am referring to. When I asked her about where she thought all of the material her teacher teaches comes from she first said, "the teachers' store because some of Mrs. Frost's books say that they're from the teachers' store" (personal communication, May 17, 2016). When I queried Lexie further on this idea, she replied that Mrs. Frost gets to decide what the students learn and what they are tested on, which comes from the principal, who is told by the superintendent. There are very real power structures within our educational systems that children know and accept at a very young age.

Brooke, Emily, Ana, Sal, and Chris all referred to the hierarchy of power in their interviews regarding what teachers teach and what students learn. When we spoke about where the material, skills, and concepts come from that the students' teachers teach, the interviewees had very similar answers. Sal said, "I think it's the government tells you. Don't they like tell you, to teach them this or that?" (personal communication, May 20, 2016). Similarly, Chris stated, "Probably the US government. I think the government should give them [teachers] a whole list of things…and tell them what's mandatory they have to teach and then if they finish all those things they'll be able to do a few special things on the side" (personal communication, May 9, 2016). These boys are accurate in their understanding and their responses highlight the control that the government has over public schools. Additionally, when Chris stated that he thinks the government *should* tell the teachers what to teach, he is anthropomorphizing Foucault's theory of governmentality because he has accepted and internalized the power that the government knows what is best for its citizens.

When we spoke about where the things kids learn in school come from, the students' responses were very similar as well. Brooke, Chris, and Ana all thought the US government, or the state is responsible for what kids learn in school. "I heard my math teacher say a couple times that she's required by the state so I think the state has something to do with it" (Ana, personal communication, May 16, 2016). Emily did not refer to the government in her discussion of what students learn in school but she did reference a hierarchy of power. She thought that the association (which through further investigating I learned was the school board) gives the books that teachers should teach from. That the school board controls the superintendent who also tells the teachers what students should learn in school. Again, there are distinct ranks in power and control within schools that the students can identify, while their responses may be varied, they all agree that the teachers who are teaching the content have very little, if any control.

When it comes to the grading of the PARCC test and who is looking at the students' scores, the government again plays a large role. Four of the seven participants specifically articulated that the government is likely grading the PARCC test. Sal elaborated, "I think like people in the government. But like smart, intelligent people" (personal communication, May 20, 2016). And Gary was not absolutely sure, "Well, I think maybe the teachers and everyone who's higher than us grades them. The government or the superintendent, most likely him" (personal communication, May 12, 2016). I think the students' uncertainty speaks to the arbitrary nature of statewide testing. They are deemed high-stakes because of the consequences attached but many of the students are confused and indifferent about the PARCC. Two of the students in this study named the government as who was viewing and concerned with how the students performed on the PARCC test. Emily thought that the government would definitely be looking at her grade. And Chris thought that the government would want to see the students' scores to know how well the teachers are doing.

As previously established, public schools that received Federal Title I funding must participate in statewide, nationally-recognized high-stakes assessments. Two of the eighth grade students in this study eluded to this idea. Ana stated that "I was told that PARCC testing was kind of a big deal for Illinois" (personal communication, May 16, 2016). Brooke explained that the district would lose funding if the students did poorly on the PARCC test. Both girls are identifying a hierarchy of power in the statements. They have come to understand that the statewide yearly exams have great influence over their school. Even if they cannot determine the specifics, they are aware that authorities outside the local school are in control.

When it comes to why students have to take the PARCC test the government was again responsible for at least three of the seven participants. Both Ana and Emily believe that the state makes teachers give the PARCC and students take it. When asked do you think the school gets to pick whether or not you take it, Emily replied, "I think the government has a big influence. Like the government or the state has a big influence on that" (personal communication, May 11, 2016). As far as the PARCC test and our state are concerned, Emily is absolutely correct. Federal mandates stipulate that districts must test 95% of their students in order to receive Title I funds. Consequently, the government *does* have a big influence on that. In Gary's discussion of why students have to take the PARCC test, he again runs through the hierarchy of power in schools,

Basically it's probably the law. The people who control basically like the president tells the government then the government tells the superintendent and the superintendent tells the principal, which tells the teacher, which tells us. (personal communication, May 12, 2016)

As Gary follows this chain of command he has identified power structures in public education. He is implying that those lower in the hierarchy do not have the freedom to decide whether or not we participate in the exam. The tests are both an accepted and imminent part of what it means to be in public education. Dean (2010) explains, "The policies and practices of government... presume to know...what constitutes good, virtuous, appropriate, responsible conduct of individuals and collectives" (p. 19). The federal requirement of statewide student testing certainly is an extension of this idea. In this way, the government knows what is best for its citizens and in our case, the PARCC test is the best and most logical means of achievement data collection on students in this Midwestern state.

Technologies of the Self

According to Lemke (2001), the term government, spans both political government to forms of self-regulation in a type of continuum. This theoretical frame permits direct intervention through specific state mechanisms of control as well as the development of indirect techniques of control. There is a shifting of responsibility for social problems and life in society into individual responsibility and transforming it into an issue of "self-care" (p. 59). For example, Smythe (2015) explains that large-scale literacy assessments increasingly share their results and interpretations to individuals as well as governing bodies to explain where individuals rank in relation to others in the state or country *and* why they should invest in their own literacy education. Here, the state deems individuals responsible for their learning while simultaneously removing the state as being accountable for individuals (p. 226). It is when individuals become responsible for their own discipline and regulation that aligns with those established by governing bodies that humans invest in "technologies of the self."

As I examined the students' interviews, references to this self-care and regulation surfaced. In fact, six of the seven interviewees expressed ideas reflective of this theory. Both Emily and Chris gave examples of how they were learning and beginning to internalize the ideals of self-regulation in school. Emily said, "We're supposed to, it seems like we're supposed to take care of everything ourselves. And even if our parents mess it up or something, the teacher wouldn't believe it and we're supposed to take care of *everything*" (personal communication, May 11, 2016). Emily goes on to cite a specific example where her teacher made her feel like she had to be responsible for both herself and her parents' actions. Similarly, at one point in Chris' interview, he was discussing how he disliked that the older students get, the more homework they have. I asked him what he thought teachers could do about that and his response speaks to the ways that children are governed into their own self-regulation regarding the responsibilities of school. "I'm not very sure cause it's important that you get to know all of the subjects and you're not always going to have a teacher tell you most of the answers to it" (personal communication, May 9, 2015). Schools, as governing bodies, are most successful when students invest in their own self-care and no longer have to be disciplined.

When it came to the PARCC test itself, there were several ways that the students demonstrated "technologies of the self." Ana explained that she prepared for the test outside of school by going on a website to practice algebra concepts because she has trouble in that area and wanted to be ready. Chris, Gary, Emily, Lexie, and Brooke expressed the care that they put into taking the PARCC test either through taking their time, putting in extra effort, or trying their best. Additionally, when Brooke was discussing why she thought kids had to take the PARCC test she stated,

> Just to kind of like improve yourself, like to kind of like, you have responsibilities. Cause in the future you're going to have to take tests. And your whole life is pretty much a test. Like you're testing everything out. (personal communication, May 26, 2016)

Students learn very early that success in school is determined by their willingness to not only comply with the system but to embrace personal responsibility for their learning. Self-regulation in terms of education removes the necessity for public schools (as extensions of the government) to provide equitable education; for students are chiefly responsible for their success or failure. Similarly, Phillippo and Griffin's (2016) study found that student "participants saw themselves and their peers across the city through a lens of personal (not district) accountability and responsibility for their educational outcomes" (p. 74). Increasingly, students come to bear the sole liability for their educational outcomes.

There were several other instances where students' discussions were reflective of Foucault's idea of "technologies of the self." For example, when I asked Lexie if she was okay with taking the PARCC test she said, "I'll take it because I want to learn that if I got it wrong I want to get it right, cause I want to practice on the ones I got wrong" (personal communication, May 17, 2016). Remember, this is Lexie's first time take the test, she does not understand that she will not be receiving her score until some time the following school year nor will she actually see which test questions she missed. Regardless, her desire to learn from her mistakes is a self-regulation technique.

When Brooke was discussing her experience in the GAT program (Gifted and Talented) she spoke to an idea characteristic of "technologies of the self." She explained, "I actually like being in the GAT program because I feel like I'm taking more in but it can get difficult because it's a lot more to take in" (personal communication, May 26, 2016). The idea wanting to "take more in" is related to self-improvement. Fontaine and Luttrell (2015) explain that "These values—of being thoughtful and 'productive' about one's uses of time and aiming towards continuous self improvement—are deeply embedded in global educational policy and schooling ideologies" (p. 51). Many of the students in this study demonstrated the ways that they desire to prosper within our schools. Often, their self-care and self-improvement align with the oppressive dominant discourses of public education.

Grade Eight Theme: Resistance

Burroughs, Kearney, and Plax (1989) explain that when student resistance is examined in the literature, it is commonly characterized as disagreeable, destructive, rebellious, and negative (p. 215). Alpert (1991) elaborates, "Works on resistance describe how students react to school attempts at cultural domination in ways that often result in their exclusion from paths leading toward academic achievement" (p. 351). Traditionally, student resistance in schools is identified as the previous authors have described. I am viewing the resistance displayed by the eighth grade students in this study in a partially different light. I do agree with Alpert, that students resist for a variety of reasons, a great number of those are in opposition to the dominant ideologies that inform the many functions of public school. However, the students in this study never resisted in the negative and disruptive ways described by Burroughs et al., but nevertheless I believe they demonstrated their resistance to the statewide, high-stakes PARCC exam.

The students in this study went along, and have gone along, with the standardized testing with no outward disruptive resistance. However, this does not mean they have not resisted the administration and participation of such exams. In Alpert's (1991) study of high school students' resistance in the classroom, he characterized student resistance in three ways: reluctant participation, arguing, and resistance as conformity. I believe the last of these modes of resistance was utilized by the eighth grade participants in this study regarding the PARCC test. Alperts (1991) suggests that the students in his study paradoxically, alongside obedience and acceptance of the school's procedures, resistance also indicated a certain degree of conformity to the schooling game (p. 356). The high school students obeyed their teacher's instructions, completed assignments, and carried out all class requirements as compliance to the school's modes of formal evaluation while expressing their own concerns with rights for individual interpretation and expression (Alperts, 1991, p. 356). Similarly, the participants in this study vocalized the personal inconsequence of the PARCC test while they simultaneously explained how they put personal effort into taking it.

Similarly, Solórzano, and Delgado Bernal (2001) introduce "conformist resistance," which emphasizes the fluidity of culture insofar as students are constantly make decisions on whether to accept or reject portions or pieces of both home and school culture (as cited in San Pedro, 2015, p. 142). The students in this study maintain their identity while conforming to standardized tests. San Pedro (2015) emphasizes that "Persevering beyond or "dealing" with systemic inequities to obtain a degree provides students with the educational credentials needed to counter inequities they have experienced" (p. 142). In this way, I think that the eighth grade students in this study conform and "deal" with standardized testing measures like the statewide PARCC and district-wide MAP. They endure the tests and put personal effort into their participation, admittedly, much more effort goes into the MAP test as the consequences have greater impact upon the students.

Additionally, San Pedro (2015) explains that critical silent literacies can be used as a tool of resistance, which I think could potentially be another theory of resistance that applies to the eighth grade students in this study. To begin, San Pedro (2015) articulates that

> Silence is agentive in classrooms where teachers may be replicating imperialist practices of negation, omission, and silencing. Silence is used to shield students' identities from dominant paradigms that may be forced upon them in schools. (p. 141)

Certainly, standardized testing measures are a controlling ideology as a practice in public education, which is imposed upon students. Silence can be viewed as a transformative resistance theory that focuses on the ways students use agency as opposed to assimilation and accommodation (San Pedro, 2015,

p. 141). I am suggesting that perhaps, the students in this study chose to be silent on matters of standardized testing because they are consciously deciding not to engage with the oppressive discourse that standardized testing practices perpetuate.

The aforementioned forms of resistance are subtle and I have identified them in the students' interviews as references to the ineffectual nature of the PARCC test. To begin, all three eighth grade participants voiced that the PARCC test had very little or no effect upon them. Sal and Ana stated that they had never been affected by their statewide tests scores. Additionally, Ana noted that the scores did not matter, as a great deal of time had passed between taking the test and actually receiving her scores. Brooke agreed, "I guess they [PARCC scores] don't affect *me* at all" (personal communication, May 26, 2016). The eighth grade students are well aware that their performance on the PARCC test has no personal consequence yet they remain compelled to go along with the testing.

Additionally, Brooke noted that during her PARCC test administration her peers would say things like, "Oh, don't worry about it" and "Well, I don't care cause it's not affecting me, then I don't really care" (personal communication, May 26, 2016). Similarly, Sal mentioned that some of his peers would just "blow-off" the test (personal communication, May 20, 2016). At the conclusion of our interview, I asked Ana if there was anything else she wanted to tell me. This is what she said,

> I feel this test, so if I take this test I don't really benefit anything from it. It doesn't really give me anything to benefit from. So, I think students, usually when they realize that, they just kinda don't try as hard. And I felt myself doing that towards the end because I was like, "Oh, I'm almost done". (personal communication, May 16, 2016)

Again, I believe sentiments like these can be viewed as conformist resistance. The students are doing what they have to do but also convey their disapproval. Going along with the testing process is easier for the students than publically expressing their opposition and dissatisfaction. San Pedro (2015) articulates this idea, "In the current era, in which zero tolerance permeates school policies, there is little room for error when students outwardly display their anger, rage, or frustration with pedagogical and curricular decisions that exclude their identities and voices from schooling spaces" (p. 142). I believe the eighth grade students have been governed to accept the inevitably of statewide high-stakes testing but they do not approve of the arbitrary measure for a variety of reasons. Their resistance as conformity is evidenced by their casual participation.

Interestingly, when I asked Sal how he felt about taking the PARCC test for six school days he replied, "It was fun because you pretty much get out of other classes" (personal communication, May 20, 2016). I do not actually believe that Sal enjoyed taking the PARCC test based upon the rest of his interview. However, I think his statement is a definitive example of resistance in school. He obviously does not care for his classes, whether that be the teachers, the content, the instruction, or the work. Sal would rather endure a standardized exam than go to class; it's more fun. I think that is a very telling notion. Throughout most of the student interviews these seven children expressed their animosity toward the PARCC test and yet Sal thinks it is more enjoyable than going to class.

One final way that Brooke spoke to the idea of resistance was when she discussed a peer opting-out of the PARCC test. Opt-out groups exist across the country to keep parents and families informed about their rights regarding their children and their participation with standardized tests. One such group is United Opt Out whose central mission is to remove the threat of high-stakes testing in public education because they believe it is destructive to children, educators, communities, the quality of instruction in classrooms, equity in schooling, and the fundamental democratic principles on which the US is based (McDermott, 2015, p. 24). The reasoning is unclear behind why the student Brooke mentioned opted-out of the PARCC. Here is some of Brooke's speculation, "One parent in our school opted-out of taking the PARCC test for their child because they felt like their child didn't need to take the PARCC test," "I think he just felt or his parents felt that it wouldn't affect him in any way," "And he's not gonna need to go to that school [junior high] anymore so it wouldn't affect him anyway." Overall, Brooke imposed her impression of the PARCC test as ineffectual and arbitrary upon her interpretation of the student who opted-out.

To opt-out of the PARCC test is a much more conspicuous form of resistance than the ways I believe the students in this study have resisted. As an administrator of the yearly mandated testing I have never had a student or guardian opt-out or refuse the test. I was curious to know if there have been such occurrences in our school, as I have not been aware of them. The principal in our elementary building has been here for twenty-one years. Up until two years ago, when the PARCC test began in our state, no guardians had ever opted their children out of the state test. The first year of PARCC implementation one student at this school opted-out. The second school year, three students opted-out. The principal also informed me that procedurally, the parents wrote a note indicating their request, the student was presented with the test to which they had to verbally refuse, then they read silently at their seats until the testing session was over. There are no repercussions for students or families who chose to opt their children out of testing.

Resistance comes in many forms. Typically thought of as disruptive and aggressive, I think the students in this study expressed subtler means of resistance through their silence and conformity. Resistance can be manifested as transformational and productive or damaging and self-defeating (San Pedro, 2015, p. 142). I think the conformist resistance that these students practiced through their participation in the PARCC test can be seen as productive. They voiced their adverse feelings toward the test and yet put at least some effort into their performance on the test itself.

Change over Time

I have identified four ways that student responses change over time, across grades three, five, and eight: (1) student interviews decrease in length of time, (2) students are more easily able to differentiate between the standardized tests they take, (3) students exhibit less anxiety about the tests themselves, and (4) consequences of tests change from personal to more isolated. This section is in direct connection to my fourth research question guiding this study; did student responses change over time (across grades three, five, and eight)?

To begin, student interviews decreased in length of time. Third grade interviews averaged 34 minutes in length while eighth grade interviews averaged 21 minutes. Additionally, students in the younger grades seemed much more eager to talk. Eighth grade students were reserved in their responses and did not elaborate much upon follow-up questions. Younger students appeared to be more comfortable speaking with me one-on-one than the eighth grade students did. There can be several factors attributing to these differences, among them, students in third grade had a familiarity with me that the eighth grade students did not. While I did not teach any of the participants in this study, the third graders' class was directly across the hall from mine.

Another factor that likely accounted for the lack of conversation from the older students is their experience in school. I am referring to the ways that students are governed, specifically teacher-student relationships. In my experience, younger students are much more likely to strike up conversations with adults than older students. Student voice practices are not maintained nor are they developed and they are lost as students progress through the grades.

Beattie (2012) refers to this idea in her work with high school students and the utilization of student voice through school transformation efforts. One student articulated, "In high school, I am unlearning how to use my voice" (Beattie, 2012, p. 158). She goes on to explain that adolescents need to feel valued, and do relevant work. We enforce obedience, passivity, and render students voiceless at a time in their lives when they need to affirm their identity and value in the world (Beattie, 2012, p. 158). Education plays a significant role in self-identity because it is, and always has been such a prevalent component of society. I think the decrease in length of interviews is indicative of the ways that children lose their voices and become more docile in their roles as students of public education. It is significant to note that while I do believe there is evidence in this research that indicates the eighth grade students resisted testing by conforming, nevertheless they are still perceived as obedient and docile because they do in fact comply with the testing.

A second way in which student responses changed over time was that students were more easily able to differentiate between the standardized tests they take as they get older. There were many instances during the third grade interviews that I noted the student was likely confusing the MAP test and the PARCC test. At our school, these tests were administered within one week of each other. Recall, third graders experienced the PARCC test for the first time and tested for seven days straight. The following week they had two days to complete the MAP Reading and Math portions. For example, Lexie noted that she got a score of 399 on her PARCC test, which does not present the student with a score upon completion, the MAP test does. Emily explained to me that as she took the PARCC test and got answers correct, the new questions would be progressively more difficult. This does not happen with the PARCC test but the MAP test program does work in this way to find a student's score. I think the test confusion speaks to the prevalence of testing in school. Third graders are learning to become accustomed to the considerable amount of evaluation systems in place in public education. They are not yet able to clearly differentiate between them all, but as my research suggests they will become better at this as they progress through school.

Fifth grade students did not seem to mix up the tests nearly as much as the third graders. Occasionally, they would mistake an action like the ability to suspend a student and allow them to restart that is possible on the MAP as something that could be done with the PARCC. It is likely the fifth graders were able to differentiate between the tests more easily because as Gary noted, "I kind of like am used to the MAP more because we did that earlier" (personal communication, May 12, 2016). As students are conditioned to take these tests, they can begin to see the differences between them more clearly.

The eighth grade students knew exactly what the PARCC was as compared to the MAP. They were able to articulate the similarities and differences among and between them without any confusion. These students have been participating in the statewide yearly exams for the past five years and the MAP test the past three in junior high school. I think the students' clear understanding of the tests by the time they got to eighth grade speaks to the hyper-surveillance of schools. Students are surveilled so much and in so many different ways that mechanisms like standardized tests become a normal, organic part of school and what it means to be a public school student.

A third way student responses changed over time was that students exhibited less anxiety about the tests themselves. It was very clear in my findings that younger students expressed their stress, apprehension, and overall nervousness much more candidly and prevalently than older students in this study. For example, I asked the students what they thought about the PARCC test and Emily, a third grader stated, "I hate it" and Sal, an eighth grader replied, "It was okay" (personal communication, May 11, May 20, 2016). The younger students were much more expressive in voicing their disdain and as the students got older their aversion to the testing, while present, was much more passive. All of the participants held adverse feelings regarding the testing but in my coding citations third grade students exemplified these ideas three times more than students in eighth grade.

Related to students exhibiting their anxiety is the fourth way that student responses change over time; consequences of tests change from personal to more isolated. As students become accustomed to the statewide yearly tests their stress decreases. This can, at least in part, be attributed to their growing understanding of the purposes of the statewide mandated test. As previously discussed in my findings, students in the lower grades commonly believed that their PARCC test scores somehow affected their grades or promotion in school. Conversely, students in eighth grade generally spoke to the notion that their PARCC scores had no personal consequence.

Older participants explained that they either were not sure what their PARCC scores were used for or if individual scores were utilized there were no personal effects. Eighth grade students have experience with the yearly state exams and have come to understand their performance does not affect their grades, placement, promotion, etc. Alternatively, students voiced that through hearsay, they have come to believe their PARCC scores affect the district. Ana noted that the test was a big deal for the state. And Brooke discussed the idea that school funding was tied to student performance on the PARCC test. As students progress through the grades, they are likely to carry less stress over taking the tests because they have learned there are limited personal consequences attached to their performance.

Summary

In this chapter I have reported the findings of my research through classroom observations, individual student's big ideas, and discussion of common overarching themes that developed through my analysis. The six common themes of standardized assessment practice in public schools that emerged in this research include: (1) adverse attitudes, feelings, and experiences with testing practices, (2) purposes and consequences of standardized assessments, (3) the ways that standardized tests are used to normalize through labeling and sorting student populations, (4) the ways in which students exhibit obedience, (5) student references to a hierarchy of power and control in schools, and (6) technologies of the self. Next, I discussed the theme of resistance, which was specific to the eighth grade participants. Finally, I identified four ways that student responses change over time, across grades three, five, and eight: (1) student interviews decrease in length of time, (2) students are more easily able to differentiate between the standardized tests they take, (3) students exhibit less anxiety about the tests themselves, and (4) consequences of tests change from personal to more isolated.

CHAPTER 8

What Does All This Mean?

> *There's so much pressure that you're putting on yourself. Plus the teachers, y'know? The PARCC and the essays, you feel like it has to be long, it has to have intelligent words in it, and it has to be perfect. Like if you don't, or accidently don't put a space or two spaces, you think, "Oh, my gosh! They're going to grade it!*
>
> EMILY (personal communication, May 11, 2016)

∴

Recapitulation

This research grew from my personal experience with standardized testing as a participant, administrator, and researcher. I set out to explore the relationship students have with standardized exams by giving them a space to have their voices heard. The many negative aspects of standardized testing from the harmful effects they have upon students and teachers, the perpetuation of the status quo, the marginalization of certain groups of students, the neoliberal forces guiding the standards movement, and many, many more inspired me to conduct this research.

As I have examined the literature regarding high-stakes standardized testing and student voice work, the intersection rarely meets. The lack of student input upon matters that concern them in the literature makes studies like this significant. McDermott (2015) articulates, "The agenda for what and who and how to teach within a public education system has been crafted by the interests of everyone it seems, except the most important and fragile of all stakeholders—children" (p. 5). Children are important, what they have to say matters and as they are governed through school they lose their agency and become docile bodies. I write this because I hope that our educational system and current practices can be altered to give students back their voices.

Students have complex relationships with the standardized testing they experience in school. Many themes emerged as I examined the data I collected, which were informed by my guiding research questions as well as the theoretical foundations of Freire's Critical Pedagogy and Foucault's Governmentality.

From these themes, I learned lessons and gathered insight into testing practices in public schools today, how students are governed, manipulated, and controlled through the standardization process, and what role student voice plays in all of this.

Conclusions

Although there is still much to be learned and understood about the ways that students express themselves regarding their perceptions and experiences with standardized testing in school, several important lessons emerged from this work. Through examination of observations and interviews I have come to understand that students are manipulated, regulated, and disciplined to view standardized testing as a natural part of what it means to be a public school student and that these mechanisms of control present themselves in many different ways. Additionally, the data I have gathered and analyzed has given me insight into the arbitrary nature of the preparation and practice students endure prior to taking these tests in school. Finally, the conversations I had the opportunity to participate in with these seven students have taught me that meaningful, deliberate, continued student voice work needs to be a part of the student experience in school, as this research has revealed that children become obedient and controlled through many different mechanisms employed in school.

The Governmentality of Assessment

Foucault's governmentality highlights not only the questions of who governs and who is governed, but also the means through which individuals' activities are shaped (Mills as cited in Hope, 2015, p. 844). Governmentality can be viewed as the 'conduct of conduct,' spanning the governing of the self to the governing of others (Gordon, 1991, p. 2). The standardized assessments utilized in public schools across the US function as a governmental mechanism of control. The data in this study has revealed that there are many ways in which students are manipulated, regulated, and disciplined to understand testing as a natural and inevitable component of their educative experience.

Over their years in school, students are manipulated into viewing standardized testing measures as both necessary and imminent. Gordon (1991) explains that individuals in our current American neo-liberal era are manipulable, they are perpetually responsive to modifications in their environment (p. 43). There are infinite ways in which students respond to their school environment. The students' assent to standardized testing is developed through their school experience. Manipulating factors that attribute to this acceptance come from teachers, administrators, the oppressive structures through which schools operate, media, peers, parents, the prevalence of examinations, the commodification of students, and market influences that penetrate schools among countless others.

In my research, this idea of manipulation is evidenced by students' gradual acceptance of yearly state exams. Students who were experiencing the flood of standardized testing for the first time tended to have very strong negative thoughts, feelings, and experiences with them. Both Emily and Lexie, the third grade participants, expressed their "hate" toward the PARCC test. These strong words were not vocalized by either the fifth nor the eighth grade students. To the contrary, as the students aged they seemed to become much more comfortable with the testing.

It was clear in the fifth grade interviews that the participants had experienced a degree of manipulation of which led them to be less vocal regarding their disdain toward the testing and they began to rationalize testing utilization in school. Both Chris and Gary, fifth grade participants, expressed that they were nervous, confused, or generally did not want to take the PARCC test. Concurrently, at different times in their interviews, the boys spoke to their acceptance of the tests. Chris and Gary felt like testing was important for a variety of reasons like being prepared for the future, getting into a "good" class or school, and self-dependence. It seemed as though these students had begun to be manipulated through various mechanisms. These students' responses differed from those of the younger participants and indicated a beginning sense of manipulation into perceiving standardized tests as a natural part of school.

The eighth grade students appeared to have endured the greatest amount of manipulation regarding the inevitability and routine existence of testing. This can certainly be attributed to the students prolonged participation in both statewide and district-wide standardized assessments as well as their maturity and understanding of school. While these students did express some feelings of nervousness or confusion they did not seem to be consuming. Alternatively, they were the most indifferent and the least worried about the PARCC test. All eighth grade students voiced that in the end, this was not a test to stress over because in actuality there were no negative personal consequences for poor performance. That being said, all eighth grade participants simultaneously explained that they put at least some effort into taking the PARCC. It is the students' passivity regarding testing that leads me to believe they are manipulated by many factors into understanding these tests as natural and part of the student experience. I think this notion is more clearly exposed because of the difference in student responses across grades 3, 5 and 8.

In addition to being manipulated, I think the students in this study have been regulated to view testing as an organic and reasonable part of what it means to be a student in public education. Students are controlled through many different technologies such as surveillance and normalization. Surveillance encourages constant monitoring of the self and others as well as disciplining individuals into specific ways of behaving to regulate populations (Hope, 2015, p. 844). One method of surveillance utilized by schools is standardized tests, which serve to regulate, discipline, and normalize individuals and populations. The students in this study demonstrate both how tests become routine and how they have been normalized by said tests.

First, the prevalence of standardized tests that the students spoke about indicates that these tests have become a natural part of the school experience. I think the pervasiveness of testing is evidenced through the students' confusion in and among the tests. The third and fifth grade students mixed up functions, formats, and capabilities between the statewide PARCC test and district-wide MAP test. The fact that they cannot distinguish one from the other implies that students are being inundated with standardization mechanisms. Soon, as established by the eighth grade participants understanding of the two tests, the students will view them as just another part of school.

Additionally, students are normalized through the standards they are tested on. Foucault's biopower includes ideas about normalizing populations. Dean (2010) states,

> All 'modern' forms of the government of the state need to be understood as attempting to articulate a bio-politics aimed at enhancing the lives of a population through the application of the norm, with the elements of a transformed sovereignty that targets subjects within a territory and whose instrument is the law. (p. 121)

Through this type of understanding holding students accountable to universal standards like the Common Core, is a means to better the nation. Adoption of the Common Core and subsequent accountability measures like the PARCC test are instruments of the law and certain methods to normalize the population.

The students in this study spoke to this notion of normalization in a variety of ways. As Foucault (1995) explains, the examination combines hierarchical surveillance and normalizing judgement to ensure disciplinary functions such as distribution and classification (p. 192). Tests like the PARCC are one such mechanism that sorts and ranks students based upon their achievement, this idea was not lost on the students in this study. All students consistently spoke to normalization through discussion of the ways that standardized tests placed them in certain classes or tracks and how they compare to their peers specifically using terms like average, below average, and above average. Education is a system that relies heavily upon controls such as standardized assessments to qualify, classify, and punish students.

Finally, I believe students are disciplined in school to see standardized testing as a natural part of school. One way that this idea was evidenced in this study was through classroom observations. Specifically, the students in Mrs. Frost's class were controlled through her discipline. They acted and behaved according to the expectations the teacher had established. Deviation was not accepted and students who did operate outside of teacher expectations were punished. The range of discipline that I observed in Mrs. Frost's class included shaming students for errors or off-task behavior, calling attention to mistakes and or misbehavior, "picking on" certain students, and making students endure repeated instruction. Students in Mrs. Frost's class have learned that they must perform as expected or there will be negative consequences.

Students in this study have been disciplined to comply with standardized testing in similar ways; do well, or else. This is especially evident for students in grades three and five. They accept the testing and want to do well because of perceived consequences. Recall, third grade students believed that the PARCC test somehow was connected to their report card grades. Foucault (1995) explains, "The distribution according to ranks or grade has a double role: it marks the gaps, hierarchizes qualities, skills and aptitudes; but it also punishes and rewards" (p. 181). The students in grades three and five noted that their scores on the PARCC test could punish or reward them. For example, Chris explained that his PARCC scores would determine what kind of college he could get into and Gary said that his scores would determine which kind of classes he would get into in junior high; if they performed poorly they would be in "lower" tracks and if they did well they would be in "higher" tracks.

Students in this study have also been disciplined into normalizing their own conduct. Hope (2015) explains that responsibilization as an element of governmentality encompasses strategies that work to remove liabilities from the state through encouraging individuals to see risks like crime, educational underachievement, or well-being as issues of self-care (851). The participants in this study demonstrate the ways that they have been disciplined to view their success or failure in school as a personal responsibility. Most students spoke about feeling pressure to do well on exams, this pressure came from school officials, parents, but mostly themselves. Additionally, students seemed to desire to do well on tests like the PARCC regardless of the consequences. They spoke about trying their best, working hard, and even taking on additional prep work outside of school.

In a world that demands transparent accountability and performance measures, schools are forced to constantly assess their student populations. I have learned through examining the data collected in this study that students are manipulated, regulated, and disciplined to view testing as a natural and inevitable part of what it means to be a public school student. Testing, reporting, ranking, and sorting kids in school is commonplace and expected. Unfortunately, there is little reflection upon what these incessant and demanding testing practices are doing to the youth. I hope the voices of the students in this study serve to open the dialogue about their experiences with these types of tests.

Wasted Time

Another important lesson that this research has revealed is the arbitrary nature of practice and preparation work students endure to get them ready for the PARCC test. The students who participated in this study are from a Midwestern suburban town. Demographically looking at the district for the 2015–2016 school year, when this study took place, 76% of students come from low-income homes, 29% are English Learners, 18% with disabilities, and 2% homeless. Large-scale standardized tests like the PARCC are not designed for these children. As Harkins and Singer (2009) explain, "Test constructors write from their own culture... [and] these tests typically measure middle or upper class experiences" (p. 80). Students in schools like ours likely do not have the cultural capital required to be successful on these types of tests, which renders their in-school prep work useless.

Kearns (2011) explores this idea of "cultural capital" in her study of standardized testing. Similar to the PARCC, she found that standardized tests produced conditions that marked marginalized youth as different than their mainstream peers. Additionally, students who failed did not have the historically dominant positions of power, specifically, the White, middle class, English, and/or male norms (p. 125). There are clear cultural, political, social, and economic norms that exist within the PARCC test and which privilege some students' cultural capital and devalue others.

The reliance upon standardized testing measures as a means and ends to student success perpetuates social inequalities. Many assessments like the PARCC claim to increase equity in schools and close the achievement gap, when in most cases the opposite is true. Students who have high achievement on these tests are privileged and those who are unsuccessful are marginalized by this systemic practice that treats all students the same (Kearns, 2011, p. 123).

We are looking at an opportunity gap rather than an achievement gap when it comes to high-stakes testing. According to the district's report card for the 2015–2016 school year there was 100% student participation; 20% met expectations, 1% exceeded expectations, and only 21.1% of our students were "ready for the next level" in terms of academic progress (illinoisreportcard.com, 2016). Despite student preparation for the PARCC test, our district has dismal performance. This correlates with the research, students whose backgrounds differ from the dominant White, upper-class, male norms will not have success with these types of tests. This is one of the contributing factors which led to my understanding that student preparation and practice in school is ineffectual.

Additionally, it was clear through the analysis of data that none of the students felt well-prepared to take the test. The interviews revealed that regardless of the time spent on PARCC practice in school or outside of school, no one considered their testing performance a success. As a collective group, most students felt like they would have liked more practice to prepare them, in terms of both format and content. Lexie thought that she would have liked more practice so that she would have known how to use the computer better. Because the PARCC is strictly administered through a computer program, students need to be able to navigate the interface, use the tools, and respond and type in acceptable ways in order to be successful, which has nothing to do with their actual understanding of the content and questions presented. Because we are a predominantly low-income school we do not have the technology of more affluent districts. The students in our district visit a computer lab once a week to work on their computer skills and when it came time to get ready for the PARCC, the computer teacher spent weekly class visits showing the students in grades 3–5 how to log onto the PARCC site and navigate the testing session. In accordance with the computer-based format for the 2015–2016 school year, our district purchased carts of Chromebooks for the students to take their PARCC tests on. Because this test relies so heavily upon the technological skills of students, those who do not have abundant opportunities to utilize the tools will be disadvantaged, namely students from low-income areas like ours.

Beyond formatting, students in this study felt like they would have liked more preparation and practice regarding the types of questions they would see on the PARCC test. Emily wished that her teacher would have told her when she was teaching things that would be on the PARCC. "I think we get most of our questions wrong because of nerves and I think she should just tell us questions are going to be on the test so you study that section of math or reading" (personal communication, May 11, 2016). I think that Emily's teacher would have told her what was on the test if she knew. The state and PARCC develop practice tests to give us an idea of what our students might see on the exams but in my experience, the tests themselves differ greatly. Again, the extra practice or emphasis upon certain areas is implemented by educators in an effort to prepare their students but most times it is done in vain as the actual tests contrast greatly.

Sal, an eighth grade student who has been participating in statewide exams for a number of years, still felt ill-prepared to take the PARCC test. He thought that there would be great benefit to taking practice tests from the beginning of the school year. These would serve as a sort-of pretest to see how students would do and then they could work on improving their performance for the actual test. I think that Sal's concern with his lack of preparation for the PARCC test speaks to the unpredictability of the exam and substantiates my argument that student preparation and practice for this test is futile.

Similarly, Chris, a fifth grade student, felt like he was not prepared to take the PARCC test. He thought that to better prepare, students in kindergarten, first grade, and second grade should be able to take the PARCC test if they want to. And if they did poorly, they could choose whether or not to have the score "count." This way students would know what to do and expect when the test does actually "count" in their future. It is very likely that if something like this were implemented, intensive state test prep in the youngest grades, we would have a population of students who had an even greater animosity toward schooling than they already do. But Chris seems to have not felt successful on the PARCC test and at least partially blames his lack of preparation.

I believe the students in this study named preparation and practice as a way to feel successful because of the ambiguity of the PARCC test. It is reasonable to think that they would have done better or at least felt better about their performance on the test if they had more practice. However, I argue that this prep work is frivolous. The students in our district are set up for failure as tests like the PARCC are not designed for them, they lack the necessary demographics to be successful. These exams perpetuate the status quo by continuously marginalizing groups and privileging others. Beyond systemic bias of testing, I believe the PARCC test itself is both uncertain and ambivalent, which means any attempts at preparing students to take the test are a waste of time.

The Urgency of Student Voice

The final lesson that I have learned through my analysis of the data is that meaningful, deliberate, and continued student voice work needs to be a part of the student experience in school, as this research has revealed; children become obedient and controlled through many different mechanisms employed in school. Student voice has been a foundational aspect of this study as I believe children are important and can make meaningful contributions to discussions especially regarding education and their experiences in school when given the opportunity to do so. I have attempted to do just that in this study. In 1999 Reay and Williams wrote that there "is virtually no literature which engages students' perspectives because it is assumed that assessments have minimal impact on youth subjectivities or that youth concerns are merely a backdrop to the assessment process" (as cited in Kearns, p. 115). While this statement is admittedly dated, I have had the same experience in my search for literature that connects both student voice and standardized assessment, which made this work all the more necessary.

There are several factors that emerged in the student data, which led to my understanding of the urgency for student voice work in schools. The ways in which student responses change over time brought these ideas to light. To begin, third and fifth grade student participants in this study appeared to be very comfortable during the individual interviews whereas eighth grade participants were visibly more reserved. Younger students were more animated in their discussions and had a great deal to share with me, on and off-topic. Students in eighth grade spoke in more even, monotone voices, they often gave short responses and did not care to elaborate when asked.

Additionally, the length of student interviews decreased as students went up in grade. Emily's (3rd grade student) interview was forty-four minutes in duration and Sal's (eighth grade student) was nineteen. There are many factors that could play a role in the varied lengths of interviews but I believe one of them is the idea that students are governed in ways that make them lose their voices. It is clear in this research that students are manipulated, regulated, and controlled in school. Some of the mechanisms of control attribute to the ways that students unlearn how to use their voices. The very structures of school render students passive and receptive to their education. There is very little room for students to express themselves vocally or otherwise. I believe that students need to have opportunities to use their voices in school. McIntyre et al. (2005) explains that this type of work with students helps them develop their identities and individual voices and prepares young people to be citizens in a democratic society (p. 160). As students in this study progressed from grades three to eight they seemed to have lost the ability to articulate and assert their thoughts and feelings as evidenced through their abbreviated interviews and some of their seemingly uncomfortable mannerisms of speaking with me one-on-one.

Dean (1999) explains that government acts on the conduct of people, specifically how one governs the self.

> Government concerns not only practices of government but also practices of the self. To analyse those practices that try to shape, sculpt,

mobilise and work through the choices, desires, aspirations, needs, wants and lifestyles of individuals and groups. (as cited in Niesche, 2015, p. 135)

The reaches of governmentality as described above certainly affect students and the ways that they learn how and how not to express themselves in school. Very young children have active imaginations and love to speak about anything that crosses their minds with anyone who will listen. We can see these mannerisms shift as soon as students enter school. Turnipseed and Darling-Hammond's 2015 article cites a study that found 98% of children test as creative geniuses at age 5 but that number decreases to only 30% by age 10 and 12% by age 15 (p. 2). Children learn the expectations of the classroom and school and act accordingly at the expense of their creativity, voice, and autonomy. Beyond the obvious discipline and controlling aspects of school, students learn the importance of self-care. It is through self-governing that children carryout their own discipline and regulation in accordance with the educational institutions' established norms.

I believe that student voice work in school is necessary because it is imperative to prepare students as future citizens of the world who question, resist and do not become passive individuals. Accepting the inevitably of standardized assessment and other governmental controls can have damaging repercussions. I maintain that kids can and should have a more significant role in education. It is my hope that by helping students reveal their voice through research such as mine, we will find more well-informed, critical adults in our society.

Allowing students spaces to truly use their voices in school will require educators to relinquish some control, which can be a difficult endeavor. Toshalis and Nakkula (2012) offer some useful approaches to student voice and effects of student voice for teachers to consider, I have pulled excerpts applicable to the current discussion as follows:

1. The more educators give their students choice, control, challenge, and opportunities for collaboration, the more their motivation and engagement are likely to rise.
2. Adolescents, who are developing their sense of identity and ability for complex thinking, need to have the chance to affect decision making, which gives rise to greater integration of students' sense of purpose, interest, and desire.
3. Promoting student voice has been linked to elevated achievement in marginalized student populations, enhanced school reform efforts, and better self-reflection.

And perhaps most importantly,

4. At its core, student voice is the antithesis of depersonalized, standardized, and homogenized educational experiences because it begins and ends with the thoughts, feelings, visions, and actions of the students themselves (pp. 32–33).

Exploring the ways that students' responses changed over time in this study have brought to light the urgency and necessity of student voice work in school. The evidence of younger students' capabilities to converse and share great detail about their testing and school experiences as compared to older students' lack of expression is obvious. Children have great insight into the world around them we need to create spaces in our schools that not only allow but celebrate their voices.

Recommendations

Given the findings and lessons learned from this study, I recommend that future research delve further into (1) the control mechanisms employed in schools and what types of effects these may have upon students' understanding of standardized testing, (2) how educators believe they convey testing compared to their students' perceptions, and (3) how the implementation of student voice work impacts student experiences and perceptions of standardized testing. First, I think that the students in this study demonstrated ways that they have been manipulated, regulated, and disciplined to view standardized tests as part of the school experience. Exploring the many possible mechanisms of control utilized in schools could provide a deeper understanding of how children are governed into accepting the inevitability of testing. These mechanisms could possibly encompass time, activity, behavior, speech, and/or the body (Foucault, 1995, p. 178).

Additionally, I think that educators believe they convey the significance of testing in many different ways. Analyzing how teachers understand their role in the testing process and comparing that to the ways that students perceive them would offer valuable insight into the teacher-student relationship. Often what we say and what we actually mean can be misconstrued, future research could compare and contrast messages, intended messages, reception, and understanding. It would be beneficial for educators to learn how they are perceived by their students when it comes to their emphasis or lack of emphasis placed upon standardized testing. Furthermore, students would have the opportunity to express themselves in safe space and impact change.

Finally, I have emphasized the importance of student voice work throughout this study. The participants in this study strengthened my belief that this type of work needs to be happening in schools beginning early and continuing throughout the years in school in a very deliberate fashion. I think future research could explore how the use and implementation of student voice work in schools impacts students' perceptions of standardized testing. It would be interesting to see if after students engaged in student voice supported classrooms, if or how their experiences and perceptions of tests changed. The critical nature of student voice work leads me to think that students would likely be able to better articulate themselves and also feel more comfortable expressing their opinions with the interviewer, but that is for future research to determine.

Furthermore, I think future research would benefit from comparison studies in different demographic areas within this Midwestern state or across the country. It would be valuable to examine the ways that student responses might differ and coincide. It would also be interesting to note how student responses depend on specific demographics. These suggestions for future research indicate that there is still much to be learned regarding student voice and standardized assessment.

CHAPTER 9

Possibilities: Where Do We Go from Here?

> *Young children need to spend their time actively engaging in play and learning through direct experiences with materials, activities, peers and teachers. Rather than measuring school success by testing, the most reliable approach to assessing young children's learning is through ongoing observations by skilled teachers and assessments of children's work over time.*
> CARLSSON-PAIGE (2013)

∴

With all of the findings, understandings, and lessons learned, where do we go from here? Overall, I think there are many possibilities for students to resist the oppressive and punitive practice of standardized testing. As discussed in Chapter 7, I believe students in eighth grade pushed-back through their conformist resistance and silence. Niesche (2015) refers to this as Foucault's 'counter-conduct' as means of resistance to the practices and techniques of governmental forms of power such as actively not speaking about an issue like testing (p. 140). There are of course, more outspoken means of resistance one of which is choosing to opt-out of participation.

In this section, I would like to specifically address opting-out as a means to resist standardized testing measures like the PARCC test. As previously established, it is not likely that large-scale high-stakes testing will be eliminated from public schooling in the near future and I believe opting-out is an effective means through which to resist. The terminology of opt-out, in and of itself, is concerning as we have to convey in certain terms that we do not want to participate while it is taken for granted that our participation is obligatory because we do not opt-in to take the PARCC test. This idea supports the governmentality framework upon which this study was built, as standardized testing has become an acceptable and inevitable part of school.

After my discussion of opting-out and the current legislation I will offer some alternatives to standardized assessments like the PARCC test. Kearns (2011) explains that a standardized summative assessment, like the PARCC, simply measures a one-time snapshot of a student. "In contrast, assessment *for* and *of* learning gives students the opportunities to show what they know in multiple ways" (p. 124). The alternatives that I will propose are assessments *for* and *of* learning.

Opting-Out

Opting-out means many different things to many different people; even the founding members of the United Opt Out group do not share one definition. Some of the critiques of standardized assessments "are made within existing discourses of excellence and merit, others are critical of the funding patterns, and still others critique the technocratic rationality implicit in standardized tests" (Mayo, 2005, p. 359). For present purposes, opting-out will focus on refusing to participate in federal, state, or local standardized assessments whether they are high-stakes or diagnostic. Further, this discussion will centrally be concerned with high-stakes mandated assessments, like the PARCC. However, Ceresta Smith's (2015) meaning of the term opt-out is closely aligned with my perspective and warrants consideration,

> For me, it means opting out of the supremacist, patriarchal notion boosted by neoliberal ideology that the elite can completely revamp public education to meet their selfish and money-grubbing needs, and this is done by *refusing to give them the high-stakes test-driven "data" they need to perpetuate the false narrative that allows them to conduct a heist on taxpayer money, social justice, and the principles of democracy.* (p. 50, emphasis added)

It is necessary to transform the narrative surrounding students opting out of tests from one of resistance for the sake of rebellion to one of necessity and substance. There is more to the opt-out movement than the surface argument conservatives point the finger at; parents and students do not want to participate in taking these tests not because they are difficult but because the arbitrary content renders most students low achievers, which could not be further from the truth. Mayo (2005) concurs, testing resistance "has restarted important conversations in communities about the aims and practices of education, the range of knowledges students ought to know, and the forms of accountability that might better take the diversity of students and knowledges into account" (p. 359). Resistance movements like opt-out, begin to open the discourse surrounding high-stakes exams, to critically engage stakeholders, and to reflect upon such legislation.

United Opt Out across the Country

Mitra et al. (2016) conducted a study exploring the ways that state policies respond to parents seeking opt-out options and pushback from opt out organizations by analyzing the most prevalent and comprehensive source on opt-out data at the time (2014), United Opt Out (pp. 3–6). The website offers visitors "Opt-Out Guides by State," which interprets enacted and practiced law on opt-out procedures. "United Opt Out's webpage is a clear case of policy ambiguity creating a policy vacuum that is then filled by an informal, but increasingly and impressively organized, grassroots effort" (Mitra et al., 2016, p. 7). While the intentions of the group are assuredly promoting equity, social justice, and pushback against federal and state control, the findings of the aforementioned study indicate that participation in the practice of opting-out could be correlated with privilege. Common threads across families who opted their children out of standardized assessments had a strong will and strong capacity for decision making about school, which means that parents with strong social capital feel that they have the power to resist policies that do not correlate with their beliefs (Mitra et al., 2016, p. 14).

Opting out is ultimately a personal decision for anyone involved in public education. Mitra et al. (2016) report that although only 2 states have policies that allow students to opt-out of statewide testing, 45 have ambiguous policies or practices encompassing opt-out provisions, for 2 states it is entirely unclear, and only 1 state indicates that children are not allowed to opt-out ever (p. 8). While many schools and districts specify participation in high-stakes exams is mandatory, parents and guardians have the final say in what is best for their children. It is the proposed inevitability of these tests that their prevalence becomes unquestionable. Assessments like the PARCC test become a rite of passage in school, like learning how to write your name in cursive, memorizing your times tables, or giving a speech. As time goes on they become less obtrusive and more embedded in the fabric of public education. This poses a tremendous problem for not only opt-out groups but for the future of democracy.

Alternatives

While the prevalence of standardized testing measures continues to infiltrate our public schools, I am hopeful that there are spaces for change if educators are inclined to take advantage. Mitra et al. (2016) refer to these contested spaces in their investigation of opt-out policies in the United States. "We have defined this concept [contested spaces] in previous research as an educational context where ideas are shared and action is taken to challenge dominant social, political, or cultural ideologies that implicate learning and teaching in schools" (Mitra et al., 2016, p. 5). This study focused on the notion that policy ambiguity around state interpretations of federal standardized assessment policy creates contested spaces where parents and activists can navigate and design opt-out strategies (Mitra et al., 2016, p. 5). I think that this concept of contested spaces can be broadened to encompass other aspects of the new ESSA legislation.

To begin, recall the following section of ESSA (2015), "the assessments shall... involve multiple up-to-date measures of student academic achievement, including measures that assess higher-order thinking skills and understanding, which may include measures of academic growth and may be partially delivered in the form of portfolios, projects, or extended performance tasks" (S1177-25). There is a great deal of room for interpretation in the above statement. Innovative teachers, schools, districts, and states could utilize this space to transform narrow standardized testing and reveal what meaningful, useful assessment resembles. Perhaps modifications to the system could begin in a place like this. For example, let's say a district interpreted this ESSA vague statement to presume they could appropriate federally approved measures of achievement in a business development project for fifth grade students. This assignment could last several months, cross all academic disciplines, involve collaboration with peers, community members, etc. It would likely provide the students with a rich and valuable learning experience. As teachers do, they would observe, collect useful anecdotal data, and provide feedback and guidance throughout the duration of the project. If the ESSA requirement at the beginning of this discussion was interpreted in this manner and the subsequent project data used to show and measure student growth to fulfill the federal mandate the possibilities and advantages could be profound.

Sternberg's (2016) article, *Testing: For better and worse* addresses the notion that our current testing culture may be making the population smarter as evidenced by rising IQ scores but at the expense of wisdom and creativity, which is dangerous to our future (p. 66). He argues that as education has become largely preparation for testing, kids do not have opportunities to explore their creativity. According to Sternberg (2016) creativity is vital to innovation and progress and wisdom is necessary to resolve the enormous challenges the world faces (pp. 70–71). Sternberg (2016) contends that, "teachers can teach and assess students for creativity and wisdom as well as for general intelligence" (p. 71). While I tend to be wary of any assessment, I do think some of Sternberg's ideas about engaging children in discussions about real-world problems and discussing how solutions to problems may be helpful at one time and harmful in another, could potentially have great benefits (p. 71). Overall, I believe expanding students' knowledge and thinking beyond what we would find on a standardized assessment is a step in the right direction.

As Turnipseed and Darling-Hammond (2015) proclaim, accountability is more than a test score. While their argument is very narrow and focuses on the business world, I believe the overarching message is both significant and true, "our young people will need analytic and creative abilities that enable them to constantly inquire, explore, and learn both on their own and with others" (p. 2). Throughout this study, I have criticized high-stakes standardized assessment mandated by federal legislation. The question to ask then is, if these types of exams were eliminated how would students, teachers, and schools be evaluated and held accountable in public schools? For in the coming future, it is unlikely accountability measures could be eliminated, they are woven into the fabric of public education by neoliberal corporate enterprise. There are three rich accountability measures I will propose in response.

One of the most prominent alternatives to standardized testing is the portfolio assessment. According to the United Opt-Out Site (n.d.) portfolio assessment is a way to assess the whole child and is a way to reflect the authentic teaching and learning that goes on within a classroom. A portfolio should be a compilation of student work that demonstrates a child's strengths, areas of need, and goals. These pieces can be student-selected, teacher-selected, or both. The work should include all subject areas and reflect the student as a speaker, reader, listener, writer, and problem solver. The types of artifacts included are individual to each student and/or teacher and should show achievement that spans the entire school year.

Another alternative to standardized assessments are performance examinations. These are tests given to all students, based on students "performing" a certain task, such as writing an essay, conducting a science experiment, or doing an oral videotaped presentation. These performance exams have the advantage over standardized tests in that they "drive the curriculum" in a relatively progressive way. According to New Schools Venture Fund (1999),

> In Milwaukee, the assessments have encouraged teachers to focus on actual student writing rather than fill-in-the-blank work sheets. They have led to more hands-on science experiments where students actually learn the scientific process and how to reflect on and analyze data, rather than merely answer questions at the end of a textbook chapter. The oral presentations have been a useful way to get students actively involved, rather than merely listening to lectures by the teacher; they also force teachers to pay attention to oral communication skills, which cannot be

tested with a paper-and-pencil exam. The actual performance assessments, once they are scored, can become part of student portfolios.

Teachers who help write the performance assessment tasks (or prompts) learn a lot about how to develop more interesting and academically valuable projects for their students. Using performance exams can encourage teachers to use a wider range of activities in the classroom, which can enrich instruction, deepen learning, and provide detailed assessment information.

Finally, exhibitions of student work are another useful assessment as a substitute to standardized testing. An exhibition is a presentation of mastery that occurs at a climactic academic moment, such as the end of a school year or at graduation. Exhibitions are summative assessments, but the process leading up to a final exhibition includes feedback, ongoing assessment, and revision. Because exhibitions involve considerable preparation, they are most successful when adopted on a school-wide basis. Additionally, an exhibition is not something that simply occurs at the conclusion of a particular unit, detached from prior learning. An exhibition is the culmination of an extended, comprehensive period of learning. An exhibition supports student mastery of specific content and standards. Exhibitions should not be limited to the fine arts. We can and should use exhibitions to demonstrate mastery in all domains (Students at the Center, n.d.).

While it appears that for measures such as PARCC testing to be altered, the entire system must be reconstructed and although this may be true, there are certainly contested spaces in which incremental and effective change can take place on a smaller and determined scale. Working within our schools may not yield the revolutionary change desired, however it is a practical and necessary place to begin. Standardized testing measures, like the PARCC, are not only arbitrary and biased but are also inaccurate and unreliable. I adamantly believe that children are intelligent, important contributors to not only education but also society as a whole. Students have been commodified and used as pawns in the game of business and privatizing public education specifically through the implementation of standardized curriculum and corresponding high-stakes exams. While this is deeply troublesome, I find hope in both possible contested spaces within the laws and the opt-out movement.

Reflections

The accumulation of the theme findings and the lessons learned, lead me to the overall conclusion that there is a need for the development of critically thoughtful students. From the themes, it is evident that students are deeply affected by the reaches of governmentality in the school setting. Notions such as normalization, regulation, docility, obedience, and technologies of the self, emerged from the student data. Additionally, there was very little evidence of resistance to testing and none of the student participants questioned the practice of statewide achievement testing. I think that as educators, we need to work diligently to help students develop their critical consciousness, one way to do that is to allow for deliberate student voice work in our classrooms.

Students are all too often dismissed and made to feel inferior, but we need to foster student strengths and truly listen to them if we hope to have engaged global citizens when these kids grow up. Lesko (2001) maintains that "the voices of the youth cannot simply be dismissed as "irrational," or "whining" because they do not share in the institutional power of education. And that if we dismiss youth's concerns with regard to their experiences of school and schooling, we may be reproducing an 'inferior' or colonial image of adolescence as emotional, becoming, naturally dependent, and confused" (p. 173). It can be challenging for adults to hear what kids have to say, especially when it contradicts existing beliefs. But we have to advocate for this kind of work or we will continue to see students lose themselves and their voices to the powers that be.

The youth in my study help elucidate how standardized testing policy is lived and experienced by students. I have learned a great deal from the students in this study about what it means to be a kid in public school, how testing works, and what their voices sound like when I really listen. As I have argued throughout this work, high-stakes standardized tests have no place in public education. I am not defending an absence of accountability however, I am convinced that tests like the PARCC are harmful to the well-being and achievement of most kids. At the conclusion of my interview with third grader Emily, I asked her if there was anything else she want to tell me about the PARCC, she replied,

Make it stop. It's torture. (personal communication, May 11, 2016)

What are we doing to our children in the name of accountability and funding? There needs to be deeper and more thoughtful consideration of those who are the most affected by these tests when it comes to enacting legislation and policies that require them. Kids have *so* much to say…if we would just listen.

References

About PARCC. (2015). Retrieved March 9, 2015, from http://www.parcconline.org/about-parcc

About PARCC. (2016). Retrieved November 16, 2016, from http://www.parcconline.org/about/states

Albers, P., Harste, J. C., & Vasquez, V. M. (2015). Critical and multimodal literacy curricula. *Negotiating Spaces for Literacy Learning: Multimodality and Governmentality*, 115–129. doi:10.5040/9781474257138.ch-008

Alpert, B. (1991). Students' resistance in the classroom. *Anthropology & Education Quarterly, 22*(4), 350–366. doi:10.1525/aeq.1991.22.4.05x1193w

American Association of Colleges for Teacher Education (AACTE) and FAQ. (n.d.). Retrieved March 27, 2017, from http://edtpa.aacte.org/faq#51

Amrein, A., & Berliner, D. (2002). *An analysis of some unintended and negative consequences of high-stakes testing.* Education Policy Studies Laboratory, Education Policy Studies Research Unit (SEPSL-02110125-EPRU).

Atlas. (2015, July 2). *No Child Left Behind.* Retrieved October 20, 2015, from http://atlas.newamerica.org/no-child-left-behind-overview

Attick, D., & Boyles, D. (2016). Pearson learning and the ongoing corporatization of public education. *Journal of Thought, 50*(1–2), 5–19.

Batters, S. M. (2011). Care of the self and the will to freedom: Michel Foucault, critique and ethics. *Senior Honors Projects.* Paper 231.

Beasley, T. (2009). Governmentaity of youth: Beyond cultural studies. In M. A. Peters, A. Beasley, M. Olssen, S. Maurer, & S. Weber (Eds.), *Governmentality studies in education* (pp. 165–199). Rotterdam, The Netherlands: Sense Publishers.

Beattie, H. (2012). Amplifying student voice: The missing link in school transformation. *Management in Education, 26*(3), 158–160. doi:10.1177/0892020612445700

Bourke, R., & Loveridge, J. (2014). Exposing the divide between assessment and the point of learning through student voice. *New Zealand Journal of Educational Studies, 49*(2), 149–161. Retrieved from http://ezproxy.lewisu.edu/login?url=http://search.proquest.com /docview/1639632801?accountid=12073

Bragg, S. (2007). "Student voice" and governmentality: The production of enterprising subjects? *Discourse: Studies in the Cultural Politics of Education, 28*(3), 343–358. doi:10.1080/01596300701458905

Burroughs, N. F., Kearney, P., & Plax, T. G. (1989). Compliance-resistance in the college classroom. *Communication Education, 38*, 214–228.

Carlson, D. L. (2009). Producing entrepreneurial subjects: Neoliberal rationalities and portfolio assessment. In M. A. Peters, A. Besley, M. Olssen, S. Maurer, & S. Weber (Eds.), *Governmentality studies in education* (pp. 257–269). Rotterdam, The Netherlands: Sense Publishers.

Carlsson-Paige, N. (2013). *A guide for parents: Advocating for your child in the early years*. Retrieved from http://www.nancycarlsson-paige.org/ECE-Brochure-8.20.13.pdf

Carspecken, P. F. (1996). *Critical ethnography in educational research: A theoretical and practical guide*. New York, NY: Routledge.

Chesky, N. Z., & Goldstein, R. A. (2016). Whispers that echo: Girls' experiences and voices in news media reports about STEM education reform. *Journal for Critical Education Policy Studies, 14*(2), 130–157. Retrieved from http://www.jceps.com/archives/3080

Clements, M. (n.d.). Edunators—Helping teachers overcome obstacles and focus on learning. The importance of reflection in education. *Edunators*. Retrieved November 24, 2013, from http://www.edunators.com/index.php/becoming-the-edunator/step-5-reflecting-for-learning/the-importance-of-reflection-in-education

Consortium for Policy Research in Education (CPRE). (2000). Assessment and accountability in the fifty states: 1999–2000 Illinois. Retrieved from http://www.cpre.org/sites/default/files/assessmentprofile/921_il.pdf

Cook-Sather, A. (2006). Sound, presence, and power: "Student voice" in educational research and reform. *Curriculum Inquiry, 36*(4), 359–390. doi:10.1111/j.1467-873X.2006.00363.x

Cormack, P., & Comber, B. (2013). High-stakes literacy tests and local effects in a rural school. *Australian Journal of Language and Literacy, 36*(2), 78–89.

Crowder, Z., & Konle, S. (2015). Gumbo ya-ya or, what Pearson can't hear: Opt-out, standardized testing, and student surveillance. *The High School Journal, 98*(4), 285–289. doi:10.1353/hsj.2015.0013

Dean, M. (2010). *Governmentality: Power and rule in modern society*. Los Angeles, CA: Sage Publications.

DeFur, S., & Korinek, L. (2010). Listening to student voices. *The Clearing House: A Journal of Educational Strategies, Issues and Ideas, 83*(1), 15. doi:10.1080/00098650903267677

Dewey, J. (1938). *Experience and education*. New York, NY: The Macmillan Company.

Diera, C. (2016). Democratic possibilities for student voice within schools undergoing reform: A student counterpublic case study. *Journal for Critical Education Policy Studies, 14*(2), 217–235. Retrieved from http://www.jceps.com/archives/3094

Fielding, M. (2001). Students as radical agents of change. *Journal of Educational Change, 2*, 123–141.

Fielding, M. (2004). Transformative approaches to student voice: Theoretical underpinnings, recalcitrant realities. *British Educational Research Journal, 30*(2), 295–311.

Flewitt, R., & Roberts-Holmes, G. (2015). Regulatory gaze and 'non-sense' phonics testing in early literacy. In M. Hamilton, R. Heydon, K. Hibbert, & R. Stooke (Eds.), *Negotiating spaces for literacy learning: Multimodality and governmentality* (pp. 95–113). London: Continuum. doi:10.5040/9781474257138.ch-007

Fontaine, C., & Luttrelle, W. (2015). Re-centring the role of care in young people's multimodal literacies: A collaborative seeing approach. In M. Hamilton,

REFERENCES

R. Heydon, K. Hibbert, & R. Stooke (Eds.), *Negotiating spaces for literacy learning: Multimodality and governmentality* (pp. 43–56). London: Bloomsbury Books. doi:10.5040/9781474257138.ch-004

Foucault, M. (1980). Truth and power. In C. Gordon (Ed.), *Power/knowledge: Selected interviews and other writings 1972–1977* (pp. 109–133). New York, NY: Pantheon.

Foucault, M. (1981). Omnes et singulatim: Towards a criticism of 'political reason.' In S. McMurrin (Ed.), *The Tanner lectures in human values volume 2* (pp. 223–254). Salt Lake City, UT: University of Utah Press.

Foucault, M. (1981). The order of discourse. In R. Young (Ed.), *Untying the text: A post-structuralist reader* (pp. 51–78). Boston, MA: Routledge & Kegan Paul.

Foucault, M. (1982). The subject and power. In H. Dreyfus & P. Rainbow (Eds.), *Michel Foucault: Beyond structuralism and hermeneutics* (pp. 201–226). Brighton: Harvester.

Foucault, M. (1991). *The Foucault effect: Studies in governmentality: With two lectures by and an interview with Michel Foucault* (G. Burchell, C. Gordon, & P. Miller, Eds.). Chicago, IL: University of Chicago Press.

Foucault, M. (1995). *Discipline and punish* (A. Sheridan, Trans., 1977). New York, NY: Random House.

Foucault, M. (1997). *Michel Foucault: 'Society must be defended.'* New York, NY: Picador.

Freire, P. (2010). *Pedagogy of the oppressed*. New York, NY: Continuum.

Giroux, H. (2003). Public pedagogy and the politics of resistance: Notes on a critical theory of educational struggle. *Educational Philosophy and Theory, 35*(1), 5–16.

Gordon, C. (1991). Governmental rationality: An introduction. In G. Burchell, C. Gordon, & P. Miller (Eds.), *The Foucault effect: Studies in governmentality: With two lectures by and an interview with Michel Foucault* (pp. 1–51). Chicago, IL: University of Chicago Press.

Gorlewski, D. A. (2012). Using standards and high-stakes testing for students: Exploiting power with critical pedagogy. *Standardizing Effective Pedagogical Practices*, 236–250.

Gorlewski, J. A. (2012). Teaching from the test: Using high-stakes assessments to enhance student learning Using Standards and High-Stakes Testing for Students: Exploiting power with critical pedagogy, 225–235.

Graham, L. J. (2009). The special branch: Governing mentalities through alternative-site placement. In M. A. Peters, A. Besley, M. Olssen, S. Maurer, & S. Weber (Eds.), *Governmentality studies in education* (pp. 235–256). Rotterdam, The Netherlands: Sense Publishers.

Hamilton, M., Heydon, R., Hibbert, K., & Stooke, R. (2015). Introduction. In M. Hamilton, R. Heydon, K. Hibbert, & R. Stooke (Eds.), *Negotiating spaces for literacy learning: Multimodality and governmentality* (pp. 1–14). London: Continuum. doi:10.5040/9781474257138.ch-001

Harkins, M. J., & Singer, S. (2009). The conundrum of large scale standardized testing: Making sure every student counts. *Journal of Thought, 44*(1–2), 77–90. doi:10.2307/jthought.44.1-2.77

Heydon, R. (2015). Multimodality and governmentality in kindergarten literacy curricula. In M. Hamilton, R. Heydon, K. Hibbert, & R. Stooke (Eds.), *Negotiating spaces for literacy learning: Multimodality and governmentality* (pp. 57–76). London: Bloomsbury. doi:10.5040/9781474257138.ch-005

Hibbert, K. (2015). The secret of 'will' in new times: Assessment affordances of a cloud curriculum. In M. Hamilton, R. Heydon, K. Hibbert, & R. Stooke (Eds.), *Negotiating spaces for literacy learning: Multimodality and governmentality* (pp. 57–76). London: Bloomsbury. doi:10.5040/9781474257138.ch-009

Hope, A. (2015). Governmentality and the 'selling' of school surveillance devices. *The Sociological Review, 63*, 840–857. doi:10.1111/1467-954X.12279

Hout, M., Elliot, S., & Frueh, S. (2012). Do high stakes tests improve learning? *Issues in Science and Technology, 29*(1), 33–38.

Howard, T. C. (2001). Telling their side of the story: African-American students' perceptions of culturally relevant teaching. *The Urban Review, 33*(2), 131–149. Retrieved from http://dx.doi.org/10.1023/A:1010393224120

Iannone, P., & Simpson, A. (2013). Students' perceptions of assessment in undergraduate mathematics. *Research in Mathematics Education, 15*(1), 17–33.

Illinois General Assembly. (n.d.). *Full Text of SB3412*. Retrieved October 6, 2015, from http://www.ilga.gov/legislation/fulltext.asp?DocName=&SessionId=85&GA=98&DocTypeId=SB&DocNum=3412&GAID=12&LegID=80716&SpecSess=&Session=

illinoisreportcard.com. (n.d.). Retrieved March 26, 2017, from https://www.illinoisreportcard.com/District.aspx?districtId=07016127502

Illinois State Board of Education Meeting. (2014, June 18). Retrieved October 12, 2015, from http://www.isbe.net/board/meetings/2014/jun/packet.pdfs

Jolley, S. A. (2014). How have we been standardized? Let me count the ways. *English Journal, 104*(2), 80.

Jones, B., & Egley, R. (2007). Learning to take tests or learning for understanding? Teachers' beliefs about test-based accountability. *The Educational Forum, 71*(3), 232–248.

Karp, S. (2016). ESSA: NCLB repackaged. *Rethinking Schools, 30*(3), 18–19. Retrieved from http://www.rethinkingschools.org/archive/30_03/30-3_karp.shtml

Kearns, L. (2011). High-stakes standardized testing and marginalized youth: An examination of the impact on those who fail. *Canadian Journal of Education, 34*(2), 113–130.

Kincheloe, J. L. (2008). *Critical pedagogy primer* (2nd ed.). New York, NY: Peter Lang Publishing.

Leistyna, P. (2007). Corporate testing: Standards, profits, and the demise of the public sphere. *Teacher Education Quarterly, 34*(2), 59–84.

REFERENCES

Lemke, T. (2002). Foucault, governmentality, and critique. *Rethinking Marxism, 14*(3), 49–64. doi:10.1080/089356902101242288

Lesko, N. (2001). *Act your age: A cultural construction of adolescence.* New York, NY: RoutledgeFalmer.

Martin, L. H., Gutman, H., & Hutton, P. H. (1988). *Technologies of the self: A seminar with Michel Foucault.* Amherst, MA: University of Massachusetts Press.

Mayo, C. (2005). Testing resistance: Busno-cratic power, standardized tests, and care of the self. *Educational Philosophy and Theory, 37*(3), 357–363. doi:10.1111/j.1469-5812.2005.00126.x

McDermott, M. (2015). Predators, colonizers, and corporate-model reform. In M. McDermott, P. Robertson, R. Jensen, & C. Smith (Eds.), *An activist handbook for the education revolution* (pp. 1–15). Charlotte, NC: Information Age Publishing, Inc.

McDermott, M. (2015). Who we are. In M. McDermott, P. Robertson, R. Jensen, & C. Smith (Eds.), *An activist handbook for the education revolution* (pp. 17–38). Charlotte, NC: Information Age Publishing, Inc.

Mcintyre, D., Pedder, D., & Rudduck, J. (2005). Pupil voice: Comfortable and uncomfortable learnings for teachers. *Research Papers in Education, 20*(2), 149–168. doi:10.1080/02671520500077970

Merriam, S. B., & Tisdell, E. J. (2016). *Qualitative research: A guide to design and implementation* (4th ed.). San Francisco, CA. Jossey-Bass.

Miller, J. J. (2013). A better grading system: Standards-based, student-centered assessment. *English Journal, 103*(1), 111–118. Retrieved from http://ezproxy.lewisu.edu/login?url=http://search.proquest.com/docview/1442779325?accountid=12073

Millham, R. A. (2012). The race to somewhere: Experiential education as an argument for not teaching to the test. In J. Gorlewski & D. Girlewsk (Eds.), *Using standards and high-stakes testing for students: Exploiting power with critical pedagogy* (pp. 178–194). New York, NY: Peter Lang.

Minarechová, M. (2012). Negative impacts of high-stakes testing. *Journal of Pedagogy/Pedagogický Casopis, 3*(1), 82–100. doi:10.2478/v10159-012-0004-x

Mitra, D., Mann, B., & Hlavacik, M. (2016). Opting out: Parents creating contested spaces to challenge standardized tests. *Education Policy Analysis Archives, 24*(31), 1–23.

Nadesan, M. (2009). Governing autism: Neoliberalism, risk, and technologies of the self. In M. A. Peters, A. Besley, M. Olssen, S. Maurer, & S. Weber (Eds.), *Governmentality studies in education* (pp. 235–256). Rotterdam, The Netherlands: Sense Publishers.

National Comprehensive Center for Teacher Quality. (n.d.). Retrieved September 30, 2016, from http://www.maine.gov/doe/accountability/documents/meec_7-20-12_Indicators.pdf

Neill, M. (2016). The testing resistance and reform movement. *Monthly Review, 67*(10), 8–28.

New Schools. (1999, April 1). *Alternatives to standardized tests*. Retrieved March 31, 2017, from http://www.newschools.org/news/alternatives-to-standardized-tests/

Niesche, R. (2015). Governmentality and my school: School principals in societies of control. *Educational Philosophy and Theory, 47*(2), 133–145. doi:10.1080/00131857.2013.793925

One Hundred Fourteenth Congress of the United States of America. (2015, January 6). *Every student succeeds act*. Retrieved from https://www.gpo.gov/fdsys/pkg/BILLS-114s1177enr/pdf/BILLS-114s1177enr.pdf

Phillippo, K., & Griffin, B. (2016). "If you don't score high enough then that's your fault": Student civic dispositions in the context of competitive school choice policy. *Journal for Critical Education Policy Studies, 14*(2), 67–95. Retrieved from http://www.jceps.com/archives/3066

Pinkwater, D. (n.d.). *The hare and the pineapple*. Retrieved from http://usny.nysed.gov/docs/the-hare-and-the-pineapple.pdf

Ravitch, D. (2012, June 5). *The pearsonizing of the American mind*. Retrieved from http://blogs.edweek.org/edweek/BridgingDifferences/2012/06/the_pearsonizing_of_the_americ.html

Ravitch, D. (2016, January 19). *Exclusive: Lamar Alexander's staff explains ESSA: Part I*. Retrieved from http://dianeravitch.net/2016/01/19/exclusive-lamar-alexanders-chief-of-staff-explains-essa-part-1/

Reay, D. (2006). 'I'm not seen as one of the clever children': Consulting primary school pupils about the social conditions of learning. *Educational Review, 58*(2), 171–181.

Robinson, C., & Taylor, C. (2009). Student voice: Theorising power and participation. *Pedagogy, Culture & Society, 17*(2), 161–175. doi:10.1080/14681360902934392

Rotherhan, A. J. (2012, May 4). What everyone missed on the pineapple question. *Time*. Retrieved from http://ideas.time.com/2012/05/04/what-everyone-missed-on-the-pineapple-question/

Salvia, J., Ysseldyke, J. E., & Bolt, S. (2017). *Assessment in special and inclusive education* (13th ed.). Boston, MA: Cengage Learning.

San Pedro, T. J. (2015). Silence as shields: Agency and resistance among Native American students in the urban southwest. *Research in the Teaching of English, 50*(2), 132–153.

Schaeffer, B. (2012). Resistance to high-stakes testing spreads. *District Administration, 48*(8), 34–42.

Schaeffer, B. (2018, February 20). *Pearson's history of testing problems*. Retrieved from http://www.fairtest.org/pearsons-history-testing-problems

Scheurich, J. (1994). Policy archaeology: A new policy studies methodology. *Journal of Education Policy, 9*(4), 297–316.

Schneider, M. K. (2015). *Common core dilemma: Who owns our schools?* New York, NY: Teachers College Press.

Schneider, M. (2016, March 18). ESSA is designed to quell opting out. It won't work [Web log comment]. Retrieved from https://deutsch29.wordpress.com/2016/03/18/essa-is-designed-to-quell-opting-out-it-wont-work/

Shepherd, B. (2015, November 24). *Bob Shepherd: Ditch the Common Core and CC tests.* Retrieved November 27, 2015, from http://dianeravitch.net/2015/11/24/bob-shepherd-ditch-coomon-core-and-cc-tests/

Shields, C. M. (2013). *Transformative leadership in education: Equitable change in an uncertain and complex world.* New York, NY: Routledge.

Smith, C. (2015). Changing the narrative. In M. McDermott, P. Robertson, R. Jensen, & C. Smith (Eds.), *An activist handbook for the education revolution* (pp. 39–56). Charlotte, NC: Information Age Publishing, Inc.

Smith, T. (2018, February, 9). *Illinois state board of education.* Retrieved from https://www.isbe.net/Documents/20180209-Letter-Future-of-PARCC.pdf

Smith, W. C. (2014). The global transformation toward testing for accountability. *Education Policy Analysis Archives, 22*(116). http://dx.doi.org/10.14507/epaa.v22.1571

Smythe, S. (2015). Beyond essential skills: Creating spaces for multimodal text production within Canada's 'minimal proficiency' policy regime. *Negotiating Spaces for Literacy Learning: Multimodality and Governmentality,* 57–76. doi:10.5040/9781474257138.ch-009

Sonu, D., Gorlewski, J., & Vallée, D. (2016). Editorial: Learn, by listening to the child in neoliberal schools. *Journal for Critical Education Policy Studies, 14*(2), 1–13. Retrieved from http://www.jceps.com/archives/3053

Staff, I. (2016, March 13). *Bell curve.* Retrieved from http://www.investopedia.com/terms/b/bell-curve.asp

Sternberg, R. J. (2016). Testing for better and worse. *Kappan, 98*(4), 66–71.

Stickney, J. (2009). Casting teachers into education reforms and regimes of inspection: Resistance to normalization through self-governance. In M. A. Peters, A. Besley, M. Olssen, S. Maurer, & S. Weber (Eds.), *Governmentality studies in education* (pp. 235–256). Rotterdam, The Netherlands: Sense Publishers.

Strauss, V. (2015, March 11). Is a new day really dawning with no child left behind's successor law? *The Washington Post.* Retrieved from https://www.washingtonpost.com/news/answer-sheet/wp/2016/03/11/is-a-new-day-really-dawning-with-no-child-left-behinds-successor-law/

Strauss, V. (2015, October 24). *Confirmed: Standardized testing has taken over our schools. But who's to blame?* Retrieved from https://www.washingtonpost.com/news/answer-sheet/wp/2015/10/24/confirmed-standardized-testing-has-taken-over-our-schools-but-whos-to-blame/?noredirect=on&utm_term=.7914fe905154

Students at the Center. (n.d.). *Student-centered assessment guide: Exhibitions.* Retrieved November 16, 2015, from http://www.studentsatthecenter.org/resources/student-centered-assessment-guide-exhibitions

Taylor, C., & Robinson, C. (2009). Student voice: Theorising power and participation. *Pedagogy, Culture & Society, 17*(2), 161–175. doi:10.1080/14681360902934392

Thomas, P. L. (2012). Using standards and high-stakes testing for students: Exploiting power with critical pedagogy. *Speaking Empowerment to Crisis: Unmasking Accountability through Critical Discourse, 425,* 45–66.

Title I—Improving the Academic Achievement of the Disadvantaged. (2005, June 21). Retrieved October 6, 2015, from http://www2.ed.gov/policy/elsec/leg/esea02/pg2.html

Toshalis, E., & Nakkula, M. (2012). Motivation, engagement, and student voice. *The Education Digest: Essential Readings Condensed for Quick Review, 78*(1), 29–35.

Tuck, E., & Gorlewski, J. (2015). Racist ordering, settler colonialism, and edTPA: A participatory policy analysis. *Educational Policy, 30*(1), 197–217. doi:10.1177/0895904815616483

Turnipseed, S., & Darling-Hammond, L. (2015). Accountability is more than a test score. *Education Policy Analysis Archives, 23,* 11. Retrieved from http://dx.doi.org/10.14507/epaa.v23.1986

United Opt Out. (n.d.). *Letter for Requesting Portfolio Assessment.* Retrieved October 26, 2015, from http://unitedoptout.com/essential-guides/letter-for-requesting-portfolio-assessment/

United States of America, Executive Office of the President. (2015, December). *Every student succeeds act: A progress report on elementary and secondary education.* Retrieved from https://obamawhitehouse.archives.gov/sites/obamawhitehouse.archives.gov/files/documents/ESSA_Progress_Report.pdf

Waxman, H. C., & Huang, S. (1997). Classroom instruction and learning environment differences between effective and ineffective urban elementary schools for African American students. *Urban Education, 32*(4), 7–44.

Xiao, Y., & Carless, D. (2013). Illustrating students' perceptions of English language assessment: Voices from China. *RELC Journal, 44*(3), 319–340. Retrieved from http://rel.sagepub.com.ezproxy.lewisu.edu/content/44/3/319.full.pdf htm

Yin, R. K. (2003). *Case study research: Design and methods* (3rd ed.). Thousand Oaks, CA: Sage Publications.

Zipin, L., & Brennan, M. (2009). Analysing secondary school strategies in changing times: The insights and gaps of a governmentality lens. In M. A. Peters, A. Besley, M. Olssen, S. Maurer, & S. Weber (Eds.), *Governmentality studies in education* (pp. 235–256). Rotterdam, The Netherlands: Sense Publishers.

Index

A Nation at Risk   16
accountability   4, 5, 8, 13, 16–21, 23, 25, 28, 37, 44, 45, 47, 86, 97, 109, 111, 119, 122, 124
adverse attitudes
  experiences with testing practices   4, 59, 76–82, 105
  feelings   77–82
autonomy   22, 68, 93, 115

biopolitics   35, 87, 109
biopower   33, 36, 87, 109

care through knowledge   34, 39–40
Carspecken, Phil Francis   49–51, 54–58, 60, 64
case study   2, 49–51, 57
change over time   53, 56, 60, 102–105, 114
Common Core State Standards (CCSS)   3, 5, 6, 17, 18, 20, 21, 38, 45
conformist resistance   63, 99, 100, 102, 118
consequences of testing   5, 22–25, 69, 70, 75, 82–86, 95, 99, 102, 104, 105, 110
control   4, 4, 21, 22, 27, 31, 33–48, 50, 51, 56, 59, 60, 63, 65, 68, 76, 86–88, 90–96, 99, 105, 107, 109, 110, 113–116, 120
critical   2, 3, 6–14, 28, 31, 34, 36, 42, 44, 49–52, 56–58, 85, 86, 99, 106, 115, 117, 119, 124
critical pedagogy   3, 6–14, 52, 106
cultural capital   111

discipline   4, 21, 33–36, 42, 44, 59, 66, 68, 87, 90, 91, 96, 97, 107, 109–111, 115, 116, 121
discourse   6, 26, 27, 30, 36, 38, 39, 41, 43, 76, 89, 98, 100, 119
diverse   2, 12, 29, 39, 57
docile   6, 42, 63, 90–92, 103, 106

education   2–24, 26–31, 33, 35, 37–40, 42–48, 52, 60, 62, 66, 68, 72, 74, 84, 86, 89–91, 93, 94, 96–99, 101, 103, 106, 109, 110, 114, 115, 116, 119–124
Education Teacher Performance Assessment (edTPA)   21
Eighth Grade   22, 53–55, 59, 66–68, 73, 80, 84, 89–91, 95, 98–100, 102–105, 108, 109, 113, 114, 118

Elementary and Secondary Education Act (ESEA)   5, 15–17
Every Student Succeeds Act (ESSA)   5, 17–20, 47, 121
exhibition   123

Fifth Grade   2, 53–55, 63–67, 70, 83, 84, 89, 103, 108, 109, 113, 114, 121
Foucault, Michel   3, 33–48, 50, 57, 86–91, 93, 94, 97, 106, 107, 109, 110, 118
Freire, Paulo   1, 6, 8–12, 52, 106

governmentality   3, 4, 33–48, 50, 51, 57, 59, 60, 72, 76, 86, 87, 93, 94, 106–111, 115, 118, 124

hierarchy of power   4, 59, 76, 93–95, 105
high-stakes testing   16, 22, 24, 45, 47, 81, 88, 100, 101, 112, 11

individualization   37, 39, 40–41, 43
interviews   1, 11, 28, 29, 50–58, 60, 68–75, 77–82, 84, 88–90, 92–94, 96, 97, 100–103, 105, 107, 108, 112, 114, 117, 124

Kincheloe, Joe L.   6–10, 12–14

lifelong learner   36, 37, 44
low-income   2, 79, 111, 112

manipulation   87, 108
mechanisms of control   33–40, 59, 86, 87, 96, 107, 114, 116
Method of Priority Observation   55, 60, 64

No Child Left Behind (NCLB), 5, 16–20, 38, 46
normalization   21, 41–43, 45, 48, 87–89, 109, 110, 124

obedience   4, 34, 59, 63, 68, 76, 90–93, 99, 103, 105, 124
observations   1, 51, 53–68, 105, 107, 110
oppression   8, 11, 12, 49
opt-out   19, 38, 101, 118–123

Partnership for Assessment of Readiness for College and Careers (PARCC)   3, 5, 17, 20–22, 24, 28, 45–48, 52, 54, 55, 71, 73, 75, 77–86, 88, 89, 91, 92, 95–104, 108–113, 118–120, 123, 124
pastoral power   34, 36, 39, 40, 43
Pearson   17, 18, 20–22, 46
performance exam   122, 123
policy   1, 5, 9, 16, 20, 1, 25, 38, 43, 47, 56, 72, 84, 96, 98, 100, 120, 121, 124
portfolio   18, 39, 40, 43, 44, 121–123
power   2, 4, 6–9, 12, 13, 19, 21, 29–31, 33–41, 43–47, 49–50, 52, 56, 57, 59, 68, 76, 87, 90, 93–96, 105, 109, 111, 118, 120, 124
purposes of testing   56, 74, 82–86, 104

Race to the Top   16
regulate/regulatory   9, 13, 33, 35–37, 59, 66, 86–88, 107, 109, 111, 114, 116
reflection   6, 9–11, 26, 31, 72, 74, 111, 115, 123–124
resistance   3, 22, 37–39, 42, 51, 56, 59, 63, 67, 68, 73, 74, 98–102, 105, 118, 119, 124

standardization   16, 13, 13, 22, 28, 42, 45, 48, 59, 60, 76, 107, 109
standardized assessment/testing   3–6, 15–17, 19, 22, 33, 44, 48, 49, 50, 52, 55, 56, 59, 69–71, 73, 74, 76, 77, 82–90, 94, 105, 107, 108, 110, 114, 115, 117–122
statewide exams   2, 3, 38, 113,
student voice   3–6, 8, 10, 11, 14, 19, 26–33, 43–49, 52, 53, 60, 76–108, 113–117, 124

technologies of the self   4, 36, 37, 39, 41–44, 59, 76, 96–98, 105, 124
test preparation   81, 92
The Coleman Report   15
Thick Record   55–57, 60
Third Grade   1–3, 24, 53, 54, 60–64, 69, 77, 78, 91, 92, 102–104, 108, 110
Title 1   19, 46, 95